THE BORN AGAIN IDENTITY

Mark A. Segraves, Ph.D.

The Born Again Identity

by Mark A. Segraves, Ph.D.

All Scripture quotations in this book are from the King James Version of the Bible unless otherwise identified.

ISBN 0-9774510-0-3

Printed in the United States by
Morris Publishing
3212 East Highway 30
Kearney, NE 68847
1-800-650-7888

To
Robin,
"Seeing you smile . . ."

TABLE OF CONTENTS

FOREWORD

Who am I? Why am I here? Does my life have purpose?

In spite of many attempts to answer these age-old philosophical challenges, they still occupy our thoughts. When I googled "Who am I," I discovered that there are 5,480,000 web sites containing this specific phrase. I'm sure they're not all concerned with deep philosophical issues (I don't have time to look at each one to see), but the sheer preponderance of the phrase indicates a cultural fascination with self-identity.

Someone said, "If you want to know who you are, go look in the mirror." That answer will probably not satisfy many people.

But what if you could find a miraculous mirror that could truly tell you who you are? Would you look into it?

There is such a mirror. It is the Word of God. (See James 1:23-25.)

In *The Born Again Identity*, Mark Segraves looks deeply into the Scriptures and discovers a rich resource of information that surpasses the best efforts of the most profound philosophers. He discovers that those who are born again have an astounding, transforming identity bound up with their identification with Christ.

In a sense, I could tell you who Mark Segraves is. I am, after all, his father. But, in another sense, his identity – and yours – goes beyond connections with human fathers. It transcends the dimensions of time and space and connects you with another Father.

You have a born again identity.

Find out who you are.

Daniel L. Segraves

CHAPTER 1
Rediscovering Your Identity

John 10:10
The thief cometh not, but for to steal, and to kill, and to destroy: I am come that they might have life, and that they might have it more abundantly.

Matthew 5:48
In a word, what I'm saying is, Grow up. You're kingdom subjects. Now live like it. Live out your God-created identity. Live generously and graciously toward others, the way God lives toward you. (The Message)

In 1980, Robert Ludlum wrote a book–recently turned into a blockbuster movie–about a man who wakes up only to realize he can't remember who he is. The rest of the story, as fast-paced and riveting as it is, revolves around his quest to answer one of the most elementary questions of life: Who am I? You may have read it–*The Bourne Identity*.

We can identify with this search for self-discovery because we've all asked the same question: Who am I? You've undoubtedly heard people (possibly yourself) say things like this: "I'm just trying to find myself" or "I'm just trying to discover who I really am!" These statements reveal the intense craving every human being has for a clear sense of identity.

Erik Erikson, the psychologist who coined the term "identity crisis," believes the struggle for identity is the most important conflict human beings encounter when they go through eight developmental stages in life. According to Erikson's psychosocial stages, the onset of the identity crisis is in the teenage years, and only individuals who succeed in resolving the crisis will be ready to face future challenges in life. This means a failure to resolve the identity crisis could very well result in perpetual struggles through the individual's life. Unfortunately, even if the crisis is successfully resolved, it may well be recurring, as the changing world around us demands that we constantly redefine ourselves.

So many people are still left asking the question: Who am I? The answer to this question is vitally important, because your perception of who you are impacts your life in numerous ways, including: 1) your approach to God; 2) the way you live your life in the blessing and power of God; 3) your perception of your purpose and mission in this world; and, ultimately, 4) your understanding of who God is.

Without a clear understanding of who you are, you will often approach God ineffectively. Instead of coming to God as one of His children—a child who has a right to "come boldly unto the throne of grace" (Hebrews 4:16)—you might approach him as a slave. It is not unbiblical to consider yourself a servant of God. Paul certainly did (Romans 1:1; Philippians 1:1; Titus 1:1) and Peter encouraged all Christians to do the same (1 Peter 2:16). But there is a radical difference between considering yourself a servant of God in the sense that you want to submit to His plan for your life and be led by His Spirit and thinking of yourself as a slave with no right to be in His presence. Most believers would emphatically deny such a perception of themselves, but their actions reveal otherwise.

Without a clear understanding of who you are, you will not be able to fully appropriate the blessings of God, perhaps because you feel like you don't deserve them. This is not the "God-wants-you-to-be-rich" prosperity-babble so prevalent today. It is truly God's desire to bless His people and He longs to demonstrate His power in our lives (2 Chronicles 16:9), but if you've lost the sense that you are indeed one of His people, you will end up living far below your privilege as a child of God.

Without a clear understanding of who you are, your perception of your purpose and mission in this world will be skewed. You will eventually forget who you are and be tempted to buy into a false, purposeless identity. But God does have a plan for you. He has a purpose for your life. "For I know the plans I have for you," declares the LORD, "plans to prosper you and not to harm you, plans to give you hope and a future" (Jeremiah 29:11, NIV). Grasping who you are is vital because your purpose is related directly to your identity.

Without a clear understanding of who you are, you will ultimately see God inaccurately and limit your ability to enter into an intimate relationship with Him. In psychological terms, projection is a defense mechanism whereby we assume others share our thoughts or feelings. This happens frequently in our walk with God. We have an acute awareness of our faults. Like David, our sin stares us in the face (Psalm 51:3) and we feel shame and guilt, and, to some degree, this is appropriate. But how many times have you asked God to forgive you of some sin and later found yourself still feeling guilty or that God was angry with you? You know in your head that the cross of Jesus Christ provided forgiveness for every sin and you've probably obsessed over your application of 1 John 1:7-10, but there is still a nagging suspicion that God is angry. The truth is that you are angry at yourself! If you approached God in faith and confessed your sin, it has been washed away and God has no awareness of it. You are simply assuming that God feels about you the way you feel about yourself! This misconception will cause you nothing but problems and intimacy with God will be next to impossible.

As you can see, it is absolutely imperative that we rediscover our identity! I've come to realize that most of the time we struggle with our faith it's not because we've forgotten who God is. It is because we have forgotten who God has declared us to be. We know all too well the magnitude of our failures. We are uncomfortably aware of our inadequacies. We know the reality of our weaknesses and that knowledge causes us to frequently forget our God-granted identity: *The Born Again Identity*.

To rediscover our identity, it is first necessary to realize how easy it is to lose and what forces might be at work to promote its loss. In the next few pages we will consider the problem of identity theft, a contemporary yet ancient problem for believers. When it comes to our identity, we need to constantly remind ourselves that one of the thief's primary purposes is to steal (John 10:10).

The Crisis of Identity Theft

Let me share something with you from the Federal Trade Commission, published on September 3, 2003.

> The Federal Trade Commission today released a survey showing that 27.3 million Americans have been victims of identity theft in the last five years, including 9.9 million people in the last year alone. According to the survey, last year's identity theft losses to businesses and financial institutions totaled nearly $48 billion and consumer victims reported $5 billion in out-of-pocket expenses. The agency also released a Commission report detailing its ID theft program since its inception.
>
> "These numbers are the real thing," said Howard Beales, Director of the FTC's Bureau of Consumer Protection. *"For several years we have been seeing anecdotal evidence that identity theft is a significant problem that is on the rise. Now we know. It is affecting millions of consumers and costing billions of dollars.* (FTC)

It is increasingly clear that identity theft is a growing problem. The technological advances of the past twenty years may include heightened security protocols, but today's criminals tend to be more sophisticated, with computer savvy that would make Bill Gates envious. Today's victims are shocked when they discover a name-less, faceless perpetrator has stolen their identity and often find their lives turned upside down even though the robbery may have been initially undetected.

The Impact of Identity Theft

I know what it's like to be robbed. Robin and I moved to Hawaii in August 2001 and we decided it would be best to put all of our belongings in storage. When my grandfather passed away later that year, we flew back to California to attend the funeral and while we were in Stockton we went by the storage facility. Everything was as it should be. We shifted some furniture around, moving a beautiful bedroom set out of the space for a few minutes and then returning it once we had found a couple of items we were looking for. I hardly noticed the people standing near their car several spaces away. Two months later we moved back to Stockton. When we found a place to stay we decided to get some of our things out of storage to help us reacquire that sense of home that often accompanies familiar things. When we arrived at our space I noticed the padlock on the door was completely different than the one I had originally used. I immediately felt sick, but I tried to minimize the situation by telling myself that someone must have banged into the door with their vehicle and the storage facility felt it necessary to put a different padlock on the door. When I went to the office they had no idea anything was different. My nausea grew. The woman behind the desk found a large pair of bolt-cutters and followed me to the space. In a moment I had the padlock off and breathlessly began to lift the roll-up door. Empty. Well, almost empty. The thieves had left a small box of paperback books—I guess they were illiterate. But there was nothing else. No luxurious bedroom set purchased with an early inheritance from my wife's grandmother. No cedar hope chest cherished by my wife for almost two decades since her grandfather had given it to her. No wedding pictures! Nothing. My wife began to shake and her eyes filled with tears. I put my arms around her and tried to think of something positive to say. Just like the storage space, nothing!

I felt violated. They had no right do this. They took things with sentimental value. They took things with practical value. They took things I didn't truly value until I felt the loss, including all of my notes and the papers I had written in my masters degree program.

I felt exposed. They took documents with personal information—tax records, bank statements, and credit card information. That's when fear made an appearance. My mind began to conjure up all kinds of terrible scenarios, from fraudulent credit charges to extortion. Violated, exposed, and afraid. Robbery will do that to you.

Satan's primary weapon against the church is identity theft and the theft usually takes place in the mind. We simply forget who we are. When this happens, our identity from the past merges with our perception of who we are in the present and we lose sight of who God has declared us to be. When we forget, we walk by sight instead of faith. When we forget, we are ruled by feelings instead of divine facts. When you consider the truth of these statements, it is not hard to understand why Satan would want to steal our identity. So what is the real impact of identity theft? Let me go back to the report from the Federal Trade Commission.

> Sixty-seven percent of identity theft victims-more than 6.5 million victims in the last year-report that existing credit card accounts were misused and 19 percent reported that checking or savings accounts were misused. (FTC)

Identity thieves do utilize certain personal information in nonfinancial ways, but they are primarily interested in spending money that is not theirs. The victims are usually devastated. Mari Frank (2005) said, "Not until I became a victim of identity theft did I know how devastated, overwhelmed and really frightened I could be. It was a nightmare." Several years ago, Mari received a telephone call from a creditor asking why she had failed to pay an $11,000.00 credit card bill. She didn't have a credit card from that creditor. More than $50,000.00 was spent in her name. A car was rented—and wrecked—in her name. In her words, "My carefully woven rug of financial security was pulled out from under me" (Frank, 2005). Her description of identity theft is as accurate as it is heart-rending.

> It's a vicious, largely faceless crime that takes an enormous financial and emotional toll on its victims. No one physically mugs you, robs you at gunpoint, or kidnaps you. No, this crime is hidden, insidious, -- most times you never meet your imposter. But you're still left feeling battered. Your self-image is beat up, your financial reputation is ruined, your sense of who you are is stolen, and your identity, in a manner of speaking, is taken hostage. It'll probably take you months (maybe years in the scenario where someone commits crimes in your name) before you get your good name back, and before your life returns to normal. (Frank, 2005)

It's not too hard to figure out what happens to a believer who is a victim of identity theft. You feel battered spiritually, emotionally, mentally, and even physically. Consequently, prayer is hindered, spiritual growth is stymied, and you feel unable to effectively conduct business in the kingdom of God. You were created to live with certainty about who you are. Tragically, the loss of identity may tempt you to live according to the principles of a prior identity and that is the first step back to slavery.

It is no great surprise that Satan would want to steal our identity. He knows that by stealing our identity he can limit our potential in the kingdom of God and minimize the quality of life we enjoy. The purpose of the thief is to steal our identity, kill our vision, and destroy any hope we have for a future. Jesus' purpose, on the other hand, is to give us life—not just any life, but abundant life (John 10:10) characterized by a clear sense of who God has declared us to be.

If you only receive one thing from reading the pages of this book, please get this: You are not who the enemy says you are! You are not who others say you are. You are not even necessarily who you think or feel you are. You are who God has declared you to be and God has called you to live out the brand-new identity He created for you (Matthew 5:48, *The Message*).

It really doesn't matter who or what you were in the past. Paul reminded the church at Corinth that their past had been taken care of by the cross of Jesus Christ.

> Know ye not that the unrighteous shall not inherit the kingdom of God? Be not deceived: neither fornicators, nor idolaters, nor adulterers, nor effeminate, nor abusers of themselves with mankind, Nor thieves, nor covetous, nor drunkards, nor revilers, nor extortioners, shall inherit the kingdom of God. *And such were some of you: but ye are washed, but ye are sanctified, but ye are justified in the name of the Lord Jesus, and by the Spirit of our God* (1 Corinthians 6:9-11).

To be washed means every sin you have ever committed has been cleansed and that cleansing is perpetually available for the rest of your life through the cross of Jesus Christ. To be sanctified means you have been set apart from the world and set apart unto God. To be justified means you have been placed in a position of right-standing with God. Every one of these benefits is directly connected to your new identity which is available in the name of Jesus and by the Spirit of God. Although your past may include evil intentions, immoral behavior, and vulgar words, all of that has been removed and you have been given a new identity. Paul said, "...if any man be in Christ, he is a new creature: old things are passed away; behold, all things are become new" (2 Corinthians 5:17). It is as simple as it is clear. If you are born again, you have been given a new identity—the born again identity!

You may not have a new name on your driver's license. You may not have a new social security number. You may still have the same bills, the same debt, and maybe even some of the same habits you had before coming to the Lord, but there is no question: You are not the same person! You have been given a new identity—a God-created identity—and the enemy of your soul will do anything to steal it away from you! In most cases, he succeeds in stealing our identity in the simplest way.

The Method of Identity Theft

Identity theft can happen in any number of ways and Robin and I have been the victims of several! For example, our bankcard number was stolen at the same restaurant... twice! Whoever wrote down the number purchased several hundreds of dollars worth of prepaid phone cards. Fortunately, the bank determined the purchases were fraudulent and reimbursed our account. There really wasn't much we could do to prevent the theft of our bankcard number (other than using cash), but the next theft was completely my fault. I was up late one night working on our bills. After writing out several checks and preparing the envelopes, I walked to our roadside mailbox, inserted the mail, and lifted the red flag. It was 2:00 a.m.

Sometime during the night they came. Before my bleary eyes opened the next morning, they were going through our credit card statements and examining our checks to determine our bank account number, routing number, and whether they could copy my conveniently provided signature.

Computer databases, containing extremely sensitive information, are hacked on a daily basis. Just yesterday, I heard a news reporter describe the newest form of computer hacking: acoustical theft. Purportedly, hackers can listen solely to the tapping of a computer keyboard and decipher screen names, passwords, and other supposedly secure information. Of course, some identity thieves aren't so clever. They'll go through your trash to find what they need. But the end result is still the same!

Satan tries to steal our identity in a number of ways, but the primary method he uses to promote the loss of our identity is the very human tendency to forget. There's nothing weird about forgetting. We all forget something at one time or another and some things really don't matter. Forget a bottle of ketchup at the grocery store and it's really not that big of a deal. But if you forget some things, it can really cause problems. Forget to pay your house payment for several months and see what happens.

Trouble! Forget to pick up your child from school and see what happens. Big trouble! Forget your wife's birthday or your anniversary and see what happens! You might want to steal someone else's identity and live under an assumed name!

Satan knows if he can get you to forget your God-created identity, you will never be everything God has called you to be. You may make it to Heaven, but you won't enjoy the fullness of God's blessings on earth. You may eventually overcome the works of the devil through the power of Jesus Christ once you are glorified, but you will never live within the full spectrum of the authority and power God wants to demonstrate in this life.

Psychologists will tell you there are many reasons we forget; let me just share a few (and I won't include age). First, we forget because we want to. This is called motivated forgetting. In some cases, memories can be painful. We wish to avoid the pain, so we are motivated to forget. But pain isn't the only motivation for forgetting. We are sometimes motivated to forget because of the consequences of remembering. Our born again identity calls us to radical life change. This is not always comfortable, so forgetting is easy. Our born again identity calls us to embrace a new set of values while rejecting the world's. This is not always convenient, so forgetting is easy. As strange as it sounds, Christians sometimes forget who God has declared them to be simply because they want to!

We also forget who God has declared us to be because there are too many other things to think about. This is called distraction. Perhaps we are thinking about our problems or circumstances. Perhaps we are so busy digesting the latest rumors that we don't have time to think about who we are. There is a sound reason why Paul encouraged the church at Philippi to think only on things that were true, honest, just, pure, lovely, and of good report (Philippians 4:8).

Another reason we forget who God has declared us to be has to do with a lack of use of that knowledge. This is called decay. By failing to consistently confess the truth of God's declaration about who we are, we neglect to lock the knowledge of the born again identity into our long term memory and ultimately into our spirits.

One final reason we forget who God has declared us to be is called displacement. We take in so much new information that previously acquired information (e.g., related to the born again identity) is pushed out. Think of the hard drive on your computer. It has an enormous but finite capacity for memory. If you fill the hard drive with an operating system, programs, databases, games, and media content, eventually the hard drive will reach its memory capacity. If that happens, you can do one of two things. Stop adding new information (which may cause you to miss out on something vital) or remove previously stored information (which can be just as damaging). Of course, with a computer you can also add to the size of your hard drive, creating more room for additional information. But human beings are not so fortunate. If you constantly fill your mind with irrelevant or useless information you will eventually find your mind unable to recall information as vital as the reality of your born again identity. There's just not room to think in terms of the world's values and continue to remember who we are at the same time.

Satan will use whatever method is effective to get you to forget. If you find the ramifications of your born again identity a little uncomfortable, he will use that as a motivation for you forget. If you are easily distracted by the vicissitudes of life, he will use that to cause you to forget. If you do not take the time to consistently confess the truths of God's Word about you, he will use that to cause you to forget. If you are tempted to fill your mind with extraneous information, he will use that to cause you to forget. He will use whatever means necessary to cause you to forget your born again identity. If he succeeds, you'll end up a spiritual billionaire living like a pauper.

The Solution for Identity Theft

So, what's the solution? How do we avoid the devastation which results from identity theft? The solution can be summed up in one word: Remember!

> For we are his workmanship, created in Christ Jesus unto good works, which God hath before ordained that we should walk in them. *Wherefore remember*, that ye being in time past Gentiles in the flesh, who are called Uncircumcision by that which is called the Circumcision in the flesh made by hands; That at that time ye were without Christ, being aliens from the commonwealth of Israel, and strangers from the covenants of promise, having no hope, and without God in the world: But *now in Christ Jesus ye who sometimes were far off are made nigh by the blood of Christ*. (Ephesians 2:10-13)

> No one will get by with vandalizing God's temple, you can be sure of that. God's temple is sacred--and *you, remember, are the temple*. (1 Corinthians 3:17)

The solution to spiritual identity theft is to remember who you are! It's as simple as that. No long lines at the Social Security office attempting to obtain a new identification number. No need to cancel the credit cards or close out your bank account or apply for a new driver's license. You've just got to remember!

The enemy of your soul would like nothing more than to make you forget. Just forget you're a child of God. Just forget you're a part of a holy nation. Just forget you're a royal priest unto God (1 Peter 2:9). If the thief can get you to forget—if he can steal your born-again identity—it will alter your approach to God. It will impact how you live your life. It will impact your perception of your purpose and mission. It will impact your perception of who God is.

But God has another idea . . . remember! Remember who you are. Go beyond your feelings about yourself. Go beyond the perceptions of others. Go straight to God's Word and you will remember who He has declared you to be! Memorize it. Confess it. For example, Paul said that the "Spirit itself beareth witness with our spirit, that we are the children of God" (Romans 8:16). If you are born again, you are the child of God. That is not what I say about you. That is certainly not what Satan says about you. It might not even be something you can say about yourself. But that is exactly what God does say about you. You are the child of God!

Memorize that verse. Confess it everyday and you'll find when the thief comes to steal your born again identity, you'll be able to use the words of Paul with confidence: "*But by the grace of God I am what I am*" (1 Corinthians 15:10). You will be able to say, "I am who God has declared me to be!"

Paul taught the church at Rome the power of confession. "For with the heart man believeth unto righteousness; and with the mouth confession is made unto salvation" (Romans 10:10). This verse was written to believers. In other words, people who are already born again should make it a practice to consistently and verbally declare the truth of God's Word. By doing so, you will avoid the pitfalls of forgetfulness (motivation, distraction, decay, and displacement) and overcome the purpose of the thief.

Identity Confession

I am not who Satan says I am.
I am not who others say I am.
I am not who I think or feel I am.
I am who God declares me to be!

References

Federal Trade Commission (2005). *FTC Releases Survey of Identity Theft in U.S. 27.3 Million Victims in Past 5 Years, Billions in Losses for Businesses and Consumers.* Retrieved September 17, 2005 from http://www.ftc.gov/opa/2003/09/idtheft.htm.

Frank, Mari (2005). *From Victim to Victor: A Step-by-Step Guide for Ending the Nightmare of Identity Theft* (2nd ed.). Edinburgh, Scotland: The Porpoise Press.

CHAPTER 2
Securing Your Identity

Ephesians 4:22-24
That ye put off concerning the former conversation the old man, which is corrupt according to the deceitful lusts; And be renewed in the spirit of your mind; And that ye put on the new man, which after God is created in righteousness and true holiness.

Many believers struggle in their relationship with God and feel like they are barely making it on their journey toward heaven because their identity has been stolen. We have realized the purpose of the thief is to steal our identity, and, through that theft, to kill our vision, and destroy all hope of a future. We have realized that our greatest means of rediscovering our identity is to simply remember. But what do we do now? It is important to understand that revelation is only powerful if it is applied. So, how do we as born again Christians fully integrate this new identity into every aspect of our lives? How do we secure this identity?

To secure means to guard from danger or risk of loss. In order to fully appropriate the blessings of God and His purpose for our life, we need to do whatever is necessary to guard against the loss of our born again identity. Think of your identity in terms of a valuable possession. What would you do to guard against the theft of something you value?

Being aware that something could be stolen is one of the biggest keys in preventing theft. Several years ago, Robin and I were privileged to travel to Europe for a couple of weeks. During that time, we visited six countries and experienced the stress of international travel every time we had to go through customs. I did not want us to get stuck in a foreign country by losing our passports or money, so I took precautions some travelers may feel unnecessary. I purchased two small pouches designed to hang around the neck under the clothes and large enough to hold a passport, credit cards, and money. I was determined to prevent pickpockets from taking something so valuable from us.

If you don't want someone to rob your house, you lock the door. You lock the windows. You might even install an alarm system. You put valuables in a safe deposit box at a bank or a fireproof safe at home. In other words, you do whatever you think is necessary to make your valuables secure.

The born again identity is eternally valuable. It is worth securing! If you lose it—through theft or negligence—the impact can be devastating. Let me demonstrate this by taking you back to the first identity theft.

> And God said, Let us make man in our image, after our likeness: and let them have dominion over the fish of the sea, and over the fowl of the air, and over the cattle, and over all the earth, and over every creeping thing that creepeth upon the earth. So God created man in his own image, in the image of God created he him; male and female created he them. And God blessed them, and God said unto them, Be fruitful, and multiply, and replenish the earth, and subdue it: and have dominion over the fish of the sea, and over the fowl of the air, and over every living thing that moveth upon the earth. (Genesis 1:26-28)

Adam and Eve were created in the image of God for the purpose of enjoying an intimate relationship with Him and with each other and co-ruling over God's creation. Satan couldn't handle this.

The Bible reveals that Satan had previously enjoyed a special position in heaven and had an intimate relationship with God. His identity was directly connected to his purpose as an angel which hovered near the throne of God. But Satan forgot who he was! He forgot that he was a finite, created being living under the authority of Almighty God. He began to dream of being something other than what God had created him to be. His loss of perspective about who he really was led to pride and the rest of the story goes downhill from there.

> How art thou fallen from heaven, O Lucifer, son of the morning! how art thou cut down to the ground, which didst weaken the nations! For thou hast said in thine heart, I will ascend into heaven, I will exalt my throne above the stars of God: I will sit also upon the mount of the congregation, in the sides of the north: I will ascend above the heights of the clouds; I will be like the most High. Yet thou shalt be brought down to hell, to the sides of the pit. (Isaiah 14:12-15)

Satan knows from experience that if he can get people to forget who they are—if he can get them to try to be something other than what God has declared them to be—they will only experience pain and disappointment.

Satan's tactic was to confuse Eve about who she was—he cast doubts on her identity. Basically, he created a sense of dissatisfaction concerning who she was. "If you eat this fruit, you can be like a god who knows good and evil" (see Genesis 3:5). There are certainly other theological issues in this passage, but we must not overlook the temptation Adam and Eve faced to become something other than what God had created them to be. The results of giving in to that temptation have been catastrophic. For Adam and Eve, their desire to assume a new identity apart from God led to disobedience and separation from God.

Adam and Eve lost so much more than they supposedly gained. They lost the paradise God had designed and created for them to live in. They lost the intimacy with God they had enjoyed. They lost the freedom to come to God in confidence; in fact, they now approached Him in fear. In their desire to find a better identity, they lost the identity God had freely given them. In the end, they introduced a destructive element (sin) which has devastated every generation of human beings from that moment to now. All of this, because they decided to try on an identity God never intended for them to have.

Satan wants to steal your God-granted identity, kill off any recollection of who you are, and destroy your reason for existing. So, how can you go about securing the born again identity? How can you make it safe from the conniving of the thief? I believe it starts with the realization that the born again identity is given freely but it not automatically appropriated into every area of our existence.

> But ye have not so learned Christ; If so be that ye have heard him, and have been taught by him, as the truth is in Jesus: That ye put off concerning the former conversation the old man, which is corrupt according to the deceitful lusts; And be renewed in the spirit of your mind; And that ye put on the new man, which after God is created in righteousness and true holiness. (Ephesians 4:20-24)

This passage is written to believers—people who have been born again! So this new identity that has been given to us through Jesus Christ is not automatically appropriated into our lives; we must put off the old and put on the new! We have to do this repeatedly because the enemy never gives up. If you remember today, he'll try to make you forget tomorrow. Why would he do this? Because he knows if he can keep you from realizing who you are and why you are here, he will limit your effectiveness in the kingdom of God and in all areas of your life. Your potential will be limited. Your relationships will be damaged. Your ministry will be obstructed. We have to realize the born again identity is not automatic. So, let me ask the question again: How do we guard our new identity so that we don't lose it again?

I want to share with you five truths or spiritual keys that will help you secure the born again identity against the trickery of the thief. Think of the valuables in your house secured by a door with five locks. I realize you would probably think someone with five locks on their front door would probably be more than a little paranoid. However, the born again identity is worth protecting, so a little illustrative hyperbole is appropriate.

It is my belief that the appropriation and securing of our born again identity can be linked to the major themes of the Reformation that took place in the 1500s. With that in mind, let me share with you the five keys with which you can secure your born again identity.

In Christ Alone

If you want to secure your identity, you must first realize that it is available in Christ alone. We are a part of a culture that applauds individual achievement. Motivational seminars are filled with similar rhetoric: You can be anything you want to be. We idolize individuals for their self-sufficiency: "He's a self-made man."

Not long ago, I came across a Colorado artist named Bobbie Carlyle. She is known for creating a sculpture out of solid rock which she titled: "The Self-Made Man" (Carlyle, 2004). The sculpture depicts a man with a chisel and hammer in his hands and it looks like he is actually chiseling the rock and causing himself to emerge. Carlyle gave permission to a group called "Funding Freedom" to adopt "The Self-Made Man" as its symbol of self-reliance and the freedom philosophy. How ironic. "The Self-Made Man" was indeed made . . . by a woman! This is an accurate picture of the reality of our individualistic society. We boast of our individual accomplishments while ignoring the fact that we have nothing and accomplish nothing without the help of others.

Our born again identity does not come to us through personal achievement. It is not ours because we have pulled ourselves up by our own bootstraps. It is not ours because we have earned it or deserve it. It comes to us only through the work of Jesus Christ. If we cannot grasp this truth and apply it to our lives, we will be unable to even begin the process of securing the born again identity.

It has always been difficult for human beings to accept the work of Jesus Christ. Paul explained this to the church at Corinth.

> For the preaching of the cross is to them that perish foolishness . . . For the Jews require a sign, and the Greeks seek after wisdom: But we preach Christ crucified, <u>unto the Jews a stumblingblock</u>, and <u>unto the Greeks foolishness</u>; But unto them which are called, both Jews and Greeks, Christ the power of God, and the wisdom of God. (1 Corinthians 1:18-24)

The Jews couldn't accept the cross, because it took the matter out of their hands. They were accustomed to a system of rewards and punishments that relied solely on their own faithfulness to that system. If they failed, they expected to be cursed. But if they succeeded at keeping the law, they expected the blessings of God. Although no one had ever succeeded at keeping the law perfectly, the system still created the illusion that the individual could through perfect obedience deserve the blessings of God. The cross required the Jews to lay down their philosophy of self-reliance and depend solely on the work of someone else and this just wasn't acceptable.

The Greeks were interested in philosophical wisdom. They were more concerned with the tickling of their ears than the transformation of their hearts. It was absurd to them that wisdom could be found in the death of a Jewish carpenter on a despicable cross.

The cross may have been unacceptable to the Jews and the Greeks, but it was and is the only means to a new life and a new identity. The Jews will never find a new identity in the Law. It is only available in Jesus Christ. The Gentile world will never find a new identity in philosophy. The born again identity comes only through the work of Jesus Christ. He made the born again identity possible by paying the ultimate price for it—His life.

No other person could ever achieve the perfection necessary to acquire this new identity on their own. Paul said "all have sinned, and come short of the glory of God" (Romans 3:23). The Greek verb tenses used in this passage make for an interesting study. In simple terms, Paul is saying that we have all sinned in the past and we all continue to sin in the present. That sounds a little discouraging, but he is simply expressing the reality of our weakness and our complete inability to change ourselves without the help of God. The good news, however, is that, in spite of our problem with the sin nature, we have been "justified freely by his grace through the redemption that is in Christ Jesus" (Romans 3:24). In other words, justification comes to us in Christ alone. If you want to experience the freedom from condemnation available through the born again identity, it is in Christ Jesus (Romans 8:1). In fact, if you are in Christ, you are a "new creature: old things are passed away; behold, all things are become new" (2 Corinthians 5:17). The first key to securing the born again identity is to realize it is in Christ alone.

By Grace Alone

If you want to guard your born again identity, you must also realize it comes to you by grace alone. Paul taught that prior to the new birth the human being is "dead in trespasses and sins" (Ephesians 2:1). In other words, our spiritual condition made it impossible to accomplish anything good on our own. We desperately needed someone else to come to our rescue and inject life into our lifeless existence. “But God, who is rich in mercy, for his great love wherewith he loved us, Even when we were dead in sins, hath quickened us together with Christ, (by grace ye are saved)” (Ephesians 2:3-4). Notice the connection between the quickening, Christ, and grace. The born again identity is obtained in Christ alone and by grace alone. It has nothing to do with our abilities, financial resources, or family heritage. We are saved by grace.

The mercy of God is extended to us through the cross of Jesus and the grace of God moves us from death to life. Mercy and grace are frequently defined inaccurately. Grace is often called the unmerited favor of God, but this is probably a better definition for mercy. In other words, through mercy we are not given what we do deserve—judgment. Through grace, we are given what we do not deserve—a new identity. Paul put it this way:

> But by the grace of God I am what I am: and his grace which was bestowed upon me was not in vain; but I laboured more abundantly than they all: yet not I, but the grace of God which was with me” (1 Corinthians 15:10).

Even though Paul claimed to work harder than anyone else, he still recognized the grace of God as the source of his born again identity. For Paul, grace was not some lofty theological concept difficult to apply to the human condition. Instead, grace was an active, divine influence whereby God creates desire and provides power within us to do His will (Philippians 2:13). Consequently, anything you have done in an effort to establish or maintain a relationship with God is solely by His grace. Your faith finds its source in grace. Your movement toward God in repentance or confession is motivated by grace. Baptism in water is efficacious only by the grace of God and baptism in the Holy Spirit is possible only by the grace of God.

I once had a lengthy discussion with a denominational Christian missionary who tried to convince me that believers need not be baptized in order to be saved because baptism is a human work. I totally disagree. The desire to be baptized comes from God. The power to be baptized comes from God. The spiritual work that takes place through baptism comes from God. In other words, baptism and any other spiritual activity we participate in are possible only through the grace of God. To label any of these as human works is a misunderstanding of God's influence in our lives.

Through Faith Alone

If you want to guard your born again identity, you must also realize it is available through faith alone. It is based on the work of Christ and comes to us by grace, but it can only be appropriated to your life by faith. You can't work hard enough for it. You can't be perfect enough to deserve it. You can't offer enough money to buy it. You can't receive it because your parents or grandparents experienced it. The born again identity is not handed down like your biological family name. It must be acquired by each successive generation and that acquisition is through faith alone.

Paul said "by grace are ye saved through faith" (Ephesians 2:8). Grace is the influence of God upon us, but it is our responsibility to respond to that grace in faith. Jesus said, "And I, if I be lifted up from the earth, will draw all men unto me. This he said, signifying what death he should die (John 12:32-33). The cross of Jesus Christ initiated the universal pull of grace on the heart of every human being, but that grace must be responded to by faith. "But without faith it is impossible to please him: for he that cometh to God must believe that he is, and that he is a rewarder of them that diligently seek him" (Hebrews 11:6). If you want to please God and experience the life transformation that results in the born again identity, you must put complete and absolute trust in the work of Jesus Christ on the cross. When it comes to the born again identity, you cannot trust Jesus and self. You cannot trust Jesus and your employer. Your faith must be in Christ alone.

On Scripture Alone

The born again identity is practical in that it finds its expression in the way you live your life. But it is also theological. By that, I mean it is a theological truth which must be based on Scripture alone. The work of Jesus Christ, the principles of grace and mercy, and the necessity of faith are thoroughly addressed in the pages of Scripture. When you attempt to live out your identity without the Word of God as the foundation for your life, you will undoubtedly experience spiritual instability. For example, some people find their identity in human tradition and when their human tradition is shaken, their faith is shaken. You must base the practical experience of your born again identity on the Word of God.

> All scripture is given by inspiration of God, and is profitable for doctrine, for reproof, for correction, for instruction in righteousness: That the man of God may be perfect, thoroughly furnished unto all good works. (2 Timothy 3:16-17)

To be who God wants me to be, I must follow the principles of His word. I must see myself as He sees me because all other perspectives are skewed by the fallen nature.

There are basically four perspectives related to who you are. There is the subjective identity: who you think you are. There is the objective identity: who others think you are. There is the ideal identity: who you think you should be. Then there is what I call the authentic identity: who you really are. But I must add a fifth perspective. There is the God-created identity (Matthew 5:48). It really doesn't matter who you think you are or should be. It really doesn't matter what others think about you. What matters is what God thinks about you and the only way for you to know what God thinks about you is to look at His Word. The born again identity must be based on Scripture alone.

For God's Glory Alone

If you want to secure your born again identity, you must also realize that it has been given to you for God's glory alone. Because we did not earn it or deserve it, we have no right to give ourselves any of the credit. In fact, God often does things in such a completely supernatural way that there is no possibility that a human being could take the credit (1 Corinthians 1:29).

Our new identity has a purpose. Not only is it connected to our salvation, it also gives us the ability to glorify God in everything we do. Whether we are ascending to the heights of spirituality in prayer and fasting or sitting in a restaurant eating a steak, our born again identity brings glory to God (1 Corinthians 10:31). Through the born again identity, we offer up the doxology of the Lord's prayer: "For thine is the kingdom, and the power, and the glory, for ever. Amen" (Matthew 6:13).

Identity Confession

I am not who Satan says I am.
I am not who others say I am.
I am not who I think or feel I am.
I am who God declares me to be!

My born again identity is in Christ alone, by grace alone, through faith alone, on Scripture alone, for God's glory alone.
I am who God declares me to be!

References:

Carlyle, Bobbie (2004). *Bobbie Carlyle Sculpture*. Retrieved September 17, 2005 from http://www.bobbiecarlylesculpture.com/index.php

CHAPTER 3
Transitions

Colossians 1:12-14
Giving thanks unto the Father, which hath made us meet to be partakers of the inheritance of the saints in light: Who hath delivered us from the power of darkness, and hath translated us into the kingdom of his dear Son: In whom we have redemption through his blood, even the forgiveness of sins.

The only way to fully appropriate the blessings of God and His purpose for your life is to understand who He declares you to be. But this understanding is often clouded by the memory of our past. God is able to forget our sins (Hebrews 10:16-18), but we find this much more of a challenge. It is difficult to think of ourselves as righteous, pure, and holy when we remember the sins we committed prior to the new birth and the sins we might have committed this morning! But God has declared us to be righteous, pure, and holy in spite of our transgressions and that declaration is based on a supernatural transition.

When God created Adam and Eve, they were completely innocent. They stood before God without shame or guilt and enjoyed an intimate relationship with Him. But when they chose to rebel against God they experienced the judgment of God—a judgment He had warned them about before they ever faced temptation. The judgment involved a devastating transition. Geographically, they were forced out of the Garden of Eden and into a thorn-infested wilderness. Physically, they went from perfect health to gradual decay. Spiritually, they moved immediately from life to death. This multifaceted transition has been passed on to us through every succeeding generation (Romans 5:12, 17). Human beings still live in the wilderness even though it may be constructed with steel girders and marble. Every attempt to develop time-saving technology has backfired with people working harder and longer than ever before. Sickness, disease, and death run rampant over medical advances. Billions are spent on research related to AIDS and cancer, but we still don't have a cure for the common cold. People around the world fill their lives with appointments and activities to disguise the fact that they are spiritually dead. Thousands of years after Adam and Eve made the decision to rebel, the poison is still with us. There is only one antidote—Christ. Only Jesus could orchestrate the supernatural transition necessary to move us from a fallen earth to a heavenly city. Only Jesus could solve the problem of sickness, disease, and death and return us to perfect health and eternal life. Only Jesus could lead the way into resurrection power and include us in this glorious victory over death. If you have experienced the new birth, you have no reason to think of yourself in historical terms. You need to consider yourself in the light of a God-directed transition. You are not what you used to be. Look carefully at these verses once again.

> Giving thanks unto the Father, which hath made us meet to be partakers of the inheritance of the saints in light: Who hath delivered us from the power of darkness, and hath translated us into the kingdom of his dear Son: In whom we have redemption through his blood, even the forgiveness of sins. (Colossians 1:12-14)

According to the apostle Paul, those possessing the born again identity have been delivered (past tense) from the power of darkness and translated (also past tense) into the kingdom of Jesus Christ. This is the spiritual before and after picture of every believer. This transition is not planned for some point in the near or distant future. It has already occurred. You are already living in the kingdom of Jesus Christ. You are no longer under the dominion and authority of the kingdom of darkness. The occasional sins you commit are not evidence of a return to a previous kingdom or a previous identity. They are simply the remnants of a fallen nature which will one day be completely obliterated in the resurrection. I am not suggesting that you minimize the reality of your sinfulness. But too many believers allow their failures to twist their self-perception into a horrible caricature of sinfulness that is incongruent with God's perception of them. Instead of sin leading you down a path of guilt, shame, and depression, you should let your mistakes turn into occasions for remembering to whose kingdom you truly belong. God has transitioned you from Satan's kingdom into the kingdom of Jesus Christ. Another way of describing this transition is a comparison of darkness and light.

> But ye are a chosen generation, a royal priesthood, an holy nation, a peculiar people; that ye should shew forth the praises of him who hath called you out of darkness into his marvellous light. (1 Peter 2:9)

Before receiving the born again identity, we lived in darkness. But notice the verb tense. God has called us out of darkness and into His light. Peter agrees with Paul. The transition has already taken place if you are born again. You do not need to struggle through the Christian life, straining against darkness in an attempt to move into the light. You are already there. Jesus did that for you.

Everything from the darkness is in your past and is no longer connected to you. "Therefore if any man be in Christ, he is a new creature: old things are passed away; behold, all things are become new" (2 Corinthians 5:17). This is another great before and after picture and, again, it is seen as occurring in the past. In other words, the work is already done. God sees you in His kingdom. God sees you in His light. God sees everything in your life and, to Him, it is brand new.

Paradoxically, there is still an element of personal responsibility. The born again identity brings with it an entirely new system of values, beliefs, and behavioral characteristics, but this new system is rarely mastered in spiritual infancy. God is able to instantly remove any or all attributes of your previous identity and He frequently does. Many drug addicts and alcoholics experience immediate deliverance. In some cases, radical changes in personality are instantaneously noticed by friends and family members. But for many people, a trace of the previous identity lingers and the struggle to overcome bad habits leads to discouragement. Perhaps this dismay would be avoided if the believer understood early in his experience that the born again identity involves a certain level of personal responsibility. There are some things you must put off and some things you must put on.

> For which things' sake the wrath of God cometh on the children of disobedience: In the which ye also walked some time, when ye lived in them. But now ye also put off all these; anger, wrath, malice, blasphemy, filthy communication out of your mouth. Lie not one to another, seeing that ye have put off the old man with his deeds; And have put on the new man, which is renewed in knowledge after the image of him that created him: (Colossians 3:6-10)

> That ye put off concerning the former conversation the old man, which is corrupt according to the deceitful lusts; And be renewed in the spirit of your mind; And that ye put on the new man, which after God is created in righteousness and true holiness. (Ephesians 4:22-24)

Notice that this passage is written to believers—people who have been born again. It is clear that the transition from Satan's kingdom to the kingdom of Jesus Christ, from darkness, to light, and from death to life is a historical reality. If you have been born again, you have been given a new identity. But this new identity that has been given to us through Jesus Christ is not automatically appropriated into every aspect of our lives. We are called to consistently put off the old and put on the new! The problem is that we can't accomplish this on our own. We can't initiate it. We can't maintain it. Ultimately, we can't make it eternal. Personal responsibility is one thing. But personal effort without God's help is quite another. If you want to talk about it in terms of percentages, I believe God does about 99% of the work and we do the rest. Of course, the 1% we do is only by the grace of God. So how does this transition work, from start to finish? I think we'll find the answer in Paul's letter to the church at Rome.

> And we know that all things work together for good to them that love God, to them who are the called according to his purpose. For whom he did foreknow, he also did predestinate to be conformed to the image of his Son, that he might be the firstborn among many brethren. Moreover whom he did predestinate, them he also called: and whom he called, them he also justified: and whom he justified, them he also glorified. What shall we then say to these things? If God be for us, who can be against us? He that spared not his own Son, but delivered him up for us all, how shall he not with him also freely give us all things? (Romans 8:28-32)

In this passage, Paul provided us with a glimpse into the supernatural transition that takes place in the life of every believer. With poetic cadence, he shows the movement from foreknowledge to predestination to calling to justification to glorification.

He Foreknew

God operates within the dimensions of time and space, but He infinitely exists outside these finite parameters. This means His perspective of the timeline of human history is much different than ours. He knows the end from the beginning (Isaiah 46:10) and is able to see all events through history at the same time. Simultaneously, God can see Adam and Eve chewing, Roman soldiers guarding an empty tomb, and you reading this book. He knows everything past, present, and future. Before time ever existed, He knew what you would have for breakfast this morning. Before you were ever born, God knew how you would respond to His grace.

Through the cross of Jesus Christ, God extends grace to every individual in the world. No one is excluded. Because He is omniscient, He knows in advance how each person will respond to His grace. His foreknowledge in no way limits our freedom to choose; He simply knows us better than we know ourselves. Because He knew billions of people would respond to the call of grace, He extended an invitation to all through the work of Jesus Christ (Titus 2:11). It is God who initiates the transition by inviting you to take on a new identity.

He Predestinated

Predestination is a concept suggested by some to mean that God arbitrarily pre-selects people for salvation. There is no Scriptural support for the idea that God has extended grace to a limited number of individuals. In fact, the Scripture is quite clear as to the universal nature of the grace of God and the work of Jesus Christ. It was because He loved the world that He gave Himself for us (John 3:16). John the Baptist described Jesus accurately when he said, "Behold the Lamb of God, which taketh away the sin of the world" (John 1:29). Just to make sure we got it right, John went on to say that Jesus' work as the propitiation for sins is not limited to believers but extends to the "whole world" (1 John 2:2). This is not the language of a limited atonement.

What is often overlooked is the fact that Paul's statement concerning predestination is written to the church. Paul had no intention of leading his audience to believe God had selected some but not all of them to be saved. He was simply explaining what God's intention was for all who chose to respond to the invitation of grace. In contemporary language, Paul might have said it like this: "If you have chosen to accept the invitation of God's grace to enter into a new life, He has a purpose for you!" In fact, that purpose extends to every person who possesses the born again identity. "For whom he did foreknow, he also did predestinate to be conformed to the image of his Son" (Romans 8:29). There it is. In one verse Paul has unveiled God's eternal purpose for your life. God wants you to be just like Jesus. His plan for you has nothing to do with a new boat, a bigger house, a nicer car, or a fatter bank account. Predestination is not about career promotions and exotic vacations. Predestination is all about separation.

When we accept His invitation to a supernatural transition, He separates us in two ways. First, He separates us from the world. The reason is obvious. The world is the bridge which connects us to our previous identity. God does not want us to cross that bridge, so He separates us from it. This concept of separation, also called holiness, carries with it the idea of distinction. We are different from the world. Our born again identity involves a new way of talking, walking, and thinking. But this is only the first type of separation. He also separates us unto Himself. To be separated from the world is not enough. You must be separated unto Him. The first separation reveals the difference between the old identity and the new. The second separation involves an intimate relationship with God not possible under our old identity. One separation without the other is not possible. You cannot be truly separated from the world without an intimate relationship with God and you cannot have an intimate relationship with God unless you are truly separated from the world.

If you want to understand God's plan for your life, submerse yourself in the Gospels. Study the life of Jesus. Look at His values, emotions, actions, and words. God's plan for you is that you become just like Him.

He Called

Through His omniscience, God knew you would respond to His grace. His plan for your life is that you become just like Him. But He understands that becoming like Him is impossible on our own. No amount of will power will help you respond to the needs of people the way Jesus did. No matter how strong your desire is to be like Jesus in every area of your life, you will always fail if you try on your own. God understands His foreknowledge is not enough to accomplish your transition. He knows His purpose for your life is futile if you lack the power to follow after it. Consequently, He called you through His grace to a place of power where His purpose can be accomplished in your life.

How would you feel if you were told to go build a house, but were given no materials, no tools, no blueprint, no training, and no financial backing? You would be one frustrated builder. But calling includes impartation. God never calls someone to do or become something without giving them the power to succeed. If you have a desire to do what God has called you to do or be what God has called you to be, that desire comes from God. Furthermore, if God has given you the desire for something so great, He always provides the power to make that a reality. "For it is God which worketh in you both to will and to do of his good pleasure" (Philippians 2:13). If you have responded to the invitation of grace, God has called you and given you the power to be exactly what He has declared you to be.

He Justified

So God knew you would respond to grace. So He has a purpose for your life. So He called you and has given you power. What exactly does God do with your old identity? Simple. He eliminates it. There may be some remaining indication that you were once someone else, but the old identity has been effectively eliminated.

Think of an immigrant who moves to the United States of America. After going through a long process, the immigrant can eventually become a United States citizen. He or she will be assigned a social security number and perhaps other forms of identification in order to effectively function as a citizen. That immigrant might destroy every form of identification he or she carried from the original country signifying that there has been a transition from one country to another. But no matter how thorough the paperwork is, there may still remain evidence of a previous citizenship. The accent may never go away. Driving may include veering into oncoming lanes of traffic. The old identity is gone, but characteristics of the old identity may remain.

When God transitions us from one kingdom to another, from darkness to light, and from death to life, He eliminates our old identity through justification. Justification is a theological term describing the process whereby God declares us to be in right-standing with Him. He understands we may occasionally say things or do things the way we used to, but He has declared us justified anyway and expects us to live accordingly.

Justification is not a sham. God doesn't fake our justify-cation. He doesn't pretend that we are in right standing with Him. There is no conversation in heaven in which God tells His angels, "I know she occasionally slips, but let's just pretend she's okay!" Remember what Paul said: "And such were some of you: but ye are washed, but ye are sanctified, but ye are justified in the name of the Lord Jesus, and by the Spirit of our God" (1 Corinthians 6:11). Nothing in this statement hints at deception. You really are washed. You really are sanctified. You really are justified. Later, Paul told the church at Corinth that Jesus was made "to be sin for us, who knew no sin; that we might be made the righteousness of God in him" (2 Corinthians 5:21). God did not pretend to place the sins of the world upon Jesus. He really became sin. And God does not pretend to place the righteousness of Jesus upon you. If you are born again, you really are righteous. Justification is not something you seek to attain. Justification is something you accept by faith. Through justification this supernatural transition into the born again identity is made a present reality. But God does not intend for your new identity to be limited to the temporal realm.

He Glorified

God knew you would respond to His grace. Because of that, He has a purpose for your life—to be like Him. He has called you and imparted to you the power to accomplish this great transformation. To be successful, you needed to get rid of the old identity and through justification He took care of that for you. Now you have received the born again identity. God has declared you to be righteous, pure, and holy. That declaration is based not on the whims of a wishful deity, but upon the certain knowledge God has about your future. He is simply calling into the present what He sees in your future.

Paul taught that the entire creation is straining toward to the day when it will experience a final radical transformation (Romans 8:22). A believer possessing the born again identity does the same. The work of Christ destroyed the works of the devil (1 John 3:8), but the world is still filled with the influence of evil. This is because the work of Christ impacts the present and the future. In the present, the curse of the law has been removed (Galatians 3:13) and individuals are free to enter into the intimate relationship with God that Adam and Eve enjoyed before their rebellion. But believers still experience sickness, disease, and death. They still struggle with the temptation to sin. But one day, sooner than we might imagine, God will complete the radical transition and we will be changed from mortality to immortality (1 Corinthians 15:53). No more sickness. No more disease. No more sin. No more death. In describing this glorious transition, Paul quoted from the prophet Hosea, "Death is swallowed up in victory. O death, where is thy sting? O grave, where is thy victory" (1 Corinthians 15:55).

It is in glorification that the born again believer achieves perfect identification. While on this earth, we yield to the influence of the Holy Spirit with the goal of fulfilling our God-created purpose—to be just like Jesus. Don't be too disappointed if you rarely succeed, just determine to never give up. Because one day, perhaps in the middle of absolute normality, God will transition you from this world to the next and you will find yourself radically changed and eternally like Him. "Beloved, now are we the sons of God, and it doth not yet appear what we shall be: but we know that, when he shall appear, <u>we shall be like him</u>; for we shall see him as he is" (1 John 3:2).

Present Transitions

To fully appropriate the blessings of God and His purpose for your life, you must understand who God has declared you to be. You are not what you used to be. You are a new creation in Christ Jesus (2 Corinthians 5:17). You are not a spiritual pauper. You are the heir of God in Christ Jesus (Romans 8:17). You may not feel like it, but you are the righteousness of God in Christ Jesus (2 Corinthians 5:21). You are a member of a royal priesthood, a citizen of a holy nation, and God's personal possession (1 Peter 2:9). For you there is no condemnation (Romans 8:1). You have been filled with power and love and the spirit of fear has no supremacy over you (2 Timothy 1:7). You are more than a conqueror (Romans 8:37) and you have overcome the world (1 John 5:4). You are no longer cursed; you are blessed with every spiritual blessing (Ephesians 1:3) and every need in your life has been met (Philippians 4:19). You are the temple of God and the Holy Spirit dwells in you (1 Corinthians 3:16, 6:19). You have been created in righteousness and true holiness (Ephesians 4:24). You are steadfast, unmovable, always abounding in the work of the Lord (1 Corinthians 15:58). You are not a part of the kingdom of darkness. You have transitioned into the kingdom of light and are now an ambassador for Jesus Christ (2 Corinthians 5:20). You walk by faith, not by sight (2 Corinthians 5:7) and you are led by the Holy Spirit (Romans 8:14). You are now a partaker of God's divine nature (2 Peter 1:4) and are always triumphant in Christ Jesus (2 Corinthians 2:14). Every statement you just read comes straight from the Word of God. It is essential that you buy into everything God has declared you to be. God sees you in a much different way than you see yourself and you need to put your absolute trust and confidence in His perspective.

Gideon lived in Israel during a time of a national spiritual famine. The people of God did "evil in the sight of the Lord" (Judges 6:1) and God judged them for this. He used the Midianites to impoverish the nation and drive Israel back toward Him. Consistent with Israel's fickle faith, they eventually tired of the devastation and began to cry out to God for deliverance. Gideon's claim to fame seems to have been the ability to hide from the Midianites. On a day when he was secretly threshing wheat by a wine press, an angel of the Lord suddenly appeared to him and called him a "mighty man of valour" (Judges 6:12). This declaration is hardly congruent with Gideon's behavior, but it didn't end there. After Gideon expressed his doubt that God was even present in Israel, the angel continued: "Go in this thy might, and thou shalt save Israel from the hand of the Midianites" (Judges 6:14). Gideon responded with a faith-filled "Who, me?" "Oh my Lord, wherewith shall I save

Israel? behold, my family is poor in Manasseh, and I am the least in my father's house" (Judges 6:15). Notice his response is directly related to his perception of himself. "I'm from a poor family. In fact, I'm the least important member of a poor family!" To fully appropriate the blessings of God and His purpose for his life, Gideon had to come to grips with what God declared him to be. He would never be able to defeat the Midianites until he could look at himself like God did. He obviously succeeded in making this transition. When Gideon led his small army against the forces of Midian, he instructed them to shout, "The sword of the LORD, and of Gideon" (Judges 7:18). That doesn't sound like a self-conscious, scared farmer from a poor family. The result? The Midianites were defeated and Gideon led the people of Israel into forty years of peace.

Experiencing victory in your life is directly related to your ability to buy into God's declaration concerning your identity. You may not feel like a mighty man or woman of valor, but that is exactly how God sees you. Now who are you going to believe—Yourself or God?

Identity Confession

I am not who Satan says I am.
I am not who others say I am.
I am not who I think or feel I am.
I am who God declares me to be!

God knows me. (foreknowledge)
God has a purpose for me. (predestination)
God has given me everything I need. (calling)
God has forgiven me. (justification)
God has a future for me. (glorification)
I am who God declares me to be!

CHAPTER 4
A Child of God

John 1:10
But as many as received him, to them gave he power to become the sons of God, even to them that believe on his name.

Romans 8:14
For as many as are led by the Spirit of God, they are the sons of God.

1 John 3:1-2
Behold, what manner of love the Father hath bestowed upon us, that we should be called the sons of God: therefore the world knoweth us not, because it knew him not. Beloved, now are we the sons of God, and it doth not yet appear what we shall be: but we know that, when he shall appear, we shall be like him; for we shall see him as he is.

Jesus could be as direct as John the Baptist when it came to identifying the spiritual condition of his audience. In one conversation, the scribes and Pharisees claimed Abraham was their father (John 8:39). Jesus acknowledged their physical ancestry, but said their actions showed they weren't the true children of Abraham. The scribes and Pharisees then claimed that God was their father (John 8:41). Again, Jesus confronted this self-righteous claim and told them their deeds proved God was not their father. He then went on to tell them who their father really was. "Ye are of your father the devil" (John 8:44).

In his first epistle, John described the children of the devil as workers of unrighteousness and haters of their brothers (1 John 3:10). The world is filled with people who by their actions are clearly children of the devil. But this is not an identity human beings are forced to live with. Through the new birth, children of the devil are transformed into children of God (John 1:10; 1 John 3:1-2). But to understand the implications of being a child of God, it is necessary to go back to the beginning.

During the first five days of creation, God revealed His supernatural genius by fashioning the most wonderful things imaginable. He called forth light, planets, stars, water, land, plants, fish, and birds with His voice alone. With each new creation, God saw that it was good. The sixth started much like the fifth. God continued His creative work, fashioning every kind of land animal conceivable. But God's creative protocol took a sudden turn when He made the first human beings.

> And God said, Let us make man in our image, after our likeness: and let them have dominion over the fish of the sea, and over the fowl of the air, and over the cattle,

> and over all the earth, and over every creeping thing that creepeth upon the earth. So God created man in his own image, in the image of God created he him; male and female created he them. And God blessed them, and God said unto them, Be fruitful, and multiply, and replenish the earth, and subdue it: and have dominion over the fish of the sea, and over the fowl of the air, and over every living thing that moveth upon the earth. (Genesis 1:26-28)

By God's choice, He created mankind in His image. No other object or creature was made in the image of God. No other object or creature was blessed in this way. No other object or creature was given dominion over the works of God's hands. There was something different and special about the creation of Adam and Eve. God had called every other part of the universe into existence with His spoken word. But God formed Adam from the dust of the ground and actually breathed into him the breath of life (Genesis 2:7). God then created Eve by using one of Adam's ribs as the starting point. In other words, the creation of Adam and Eve was unique and intensely personal to God. By God's will, Adam and Eve were created in the image of God, and that image has been passed down to every succeeding generation.

The Psalmist recognized how incredible it really was:

"I will praise thee; for I am fearfully and wonderfully made: marvellous are thy works; and that my soul knoweth right well" (Psalm 139:14). In another place, the Psalmist acknowledged that man was just a "little lower than the angels" (Psalm 8:5) and had been given dominion over the rest of the created world. Why would God bless Adam and Eve and give them the task of ruling His creation? I think we can find the answer in one of several oft-neglected passages of Scripture called genealogies. I won't include it all, but I think you'll see what I'm talking about. In Luke's genealogy of the Messiah, we find these words,

> Which was the son of Mathusala, which was the son of Enoch, which was the son of Jared, which was the son of Maleleel, which was the son of Cainan, Which was the son of Enos, which was the son of Seth, which was the son of Adam, which was the son of God. (Luke 3:37-38)

Did you catch it? It's no wonder Adam was blessed, he was the son of God! No other creature could boast such a relationship with God. Adam and Eve were created in the image of God and enjoyed the incredible status of being His children.

As the children of God, Adam and Eve were given a beautiful place to live. In fact, it was a paradise. In what was probably a tropical environment, Adam and Eve could roam across grass covered knolls and sample exotic fruits of every variety, one of which guaranteed they would live forever. The weather was mild enough to sleep without shelter or clothing and animals posed absolutely no threat to their existence.

As the children of God, every need was taken care of. Food was plenteous and sustaining and rivers and streams were undoubtedly crystal clear and the water unbelievably refreshing.

As the children of God, they enjoyed an intimate relationship with God and had no trouble hearing the audible voice of the Lord (Genesis 3:8). In complete transparency, they were able to interact with God without shame or guilt.

As the children of God, they enjoyed fellowship with each other. Their relationship was pure and honest, unencumbered by confusion, conflict, or clothes!

As the children of God, they were given the task of taking dominion of the created world and together ruling as God's vice-regents. This challenging task was undoubtedly designed to provide a level of fulfillment unachievable by eating fruit salads and taking nature hikes.

There is no way to be certain about how much time Adam and Eve enjoyed these many benefits. It may have been years. It may have been a few days. From either perspective, this extraordinary existence came to a screeching halt when Adam and Eve willingly walked away from their relationship with God as His children. It doesn't make much sense. They traded all of the benefits for one bite of forbidden fruit, a bite fueled by a desire to become something different than what God had created them to be.

As a result of the sin of Adam and Eve, their existence was radically changed. They went from innocence and purity to shame and guilt. They were forced from the Garden of Eden. Adam was forced to work hard to survive and provide for his family. Eve was forced to endure pain in childbirth God had never intended. Their relationship with God was devastated, characterized by fear instead of transparency. Their relationship with each other damaged, characterized by blame (Genesis 3:9-13). Instead of dominating the created world, the created world began to dominate them. Instead of living forever, they experienced an immediate spiritual death and a progressive, relentless physical mortality.

Fortunately, God's plan for man could not be thwarted by the mistakes of His children. When Adam and Eve chose to follow the advice of another father and lost their relationship with God, He put into motion His plan to restore the human race to its rightful place as His children. If Adam and Eve had never fallen, every one of their descendents would have enjoyed a relationship with God as His child. God's intention has always been to make a way for every individual who so chooses to reenter into that relationship, and He revealed this desire soon after Adam and Eve sinned.

> And the LORD God said unto the serpent, Because thou hast done this, thou art cursed above all cattle, and above every beast of the field; upon thy belly shalt thou go, and dust shalt thou eat all the days of thy life: And I will put enmity between thee and the woman, and between thy seed and her seed; it shall bruise thy head, and thou shalt bruise his heel. (Genesis 3:14-15)

This is the first prophecy of a Messiah who would restore the human race to its rightful place as the children of God, a prophecy which was fulfilled by Jesus Christ. Through His death, Jesus took care of the sin problem and made a way for human beings to again enjoy the relationship with God as their Father.

> But when the fulness of the time was come, God sent forth his Son, made of a woman, made under the law, To redeem them that were under the law, that we might receive the adoption of sons. And because ye are sons, God hath sent forth the Spirit of his Son into your hearts, crying, Abba, Father. (Galatians 4:4-5)

Jesus' purpose for coming was to restore us to our rightful position as the children of God. You now have a choice: you can be a child of God or you can be a child of the devil. If you are born again, you are the child of God and as such you have access into innumerable blessings you might not be able to imagine. You can get a glimpse of these blessings by thinking in terms of what Adam and Eve lost.

A Heavenly Home

As the possessor of the born again identity you have been given a beautiful place to live. Jesus said,

> Let not your heart be troubled: ye believe in God, believe also in me. In my Father's house are many mansions: if it were not so, I would have told you. I go to prepare a place for you. And if I go and prepare a place for you, I will come again, and receive you unto myself; that where I am, there ye may be also. (John 14:1-3)

You may or may not live in a nice home right now, but you are guaranteed a home beyond compare in the life to come. Jesus said there were already many mansions in His Father's house, so what could He have meant by saying He was going to prepare a place for us? It must be truly amazing!

A Supernatural Provision

You may or may not have an impressive bank account or own vast estates, but if you are the child of God every need you could ever have will be taken care of (Philippians 4:19). God doesn't fail to feed the birds of the air or clothe the lilies of the field (Matthew 6:26, 28), and He has promised to take care of your every need.

An Intimate Relationship with God

Sin drove a wedge between God and man, a barrier that would not be irrevocably removed until Jesus shed His blood on the cross. But through His death, you have been given the opportunity to experience a transparent and intimate relationship with God.

> That at that time ye were without Christ, being aliens from the commonwealth of Israel, and strangers from the covenants of promise, having no hope, and without God in the world: But now in Christ Jesus ye who sometimes were far off are made nigh by the blood of Christ. (Ephesians 2:12-13)

Without the cross, you would have to view God from a distance. In fact, it would have been almost impossible to see Him. But the blood of Jesus, like a divine magnet, drew you to Him and you now can enjoy a truly intimate relationship with God.

A Restored Relationship with People

The born again identity brings with it the ability to enter into healthy relationships with other people. All of the devastating dynamics that ruin human relationships have been taken care of by the cross and if you are willing to appropriate the principles of being a child of God, you can enjoy deep, lasting relationships!

A Challenging Task

Sin has marred the created world and made it difficult to regain dominion. I doubt I will ever attempt to sleep under the stars in a field also populated by hungry grizzlies until I'm sure I'm in my glorified body. But I do know the children of God have been given a challenging task to fulfill until that day. Jesus said, "Go ye into all the world, and preach the gospel to every creature" (Mark 16:15). But don't forget about dominion; it's still going to happen. When Jesus returns, the Scripture makes it clear we will reign with Him (2 Timothy 2:12; Revelation 20:6). According to Paul, we will even have a part in judging the angels (1 Corinthians 6:3).

As you can see, everything Adam and Eve lost by sinning has been returned to us through the work of Jesus Christ. Even the tree of life, which they lost access to, will be restored to us very soon (Revelation 2:7; 22:2, 14). If you are the possessor of the born again identity, you are a child of God and you are blessed. But let's consider in more detail the implications of your relationship with God as His child.

An Eternal Inheritance

According to Paul, you are "no more a servant, but a son; and if son, then an heir of God through Christ" (Galatians 4:7). We find support for this concept in Paul's letter to the church at Rome.

> The Spirit itself beareth witness with our spirit, that we are the children of God: And if children, then heirs; heirs of God, and joint-heirs with Christ; if so be that we suffer with him, that we may be also glorified together. (Romans 8:16-17)

Two times, in two different letters, Paul said that because we are the children of God, we are His heirs. Specifically, we are joint-heirs with Jesus Christ. In human terms, an heir is an individual who is legally identified as the successor in ownership of some property or assets unless, of course, the original owner has made the decision through a will to leave the property to someone else. In spiritual terms, the children of God are designated as the recipients of all that God has (Ephesians 1:11). In fact, whatever Jesus is entitled to, every other child of God is also entitled (Romans 8:17). For now, we enjoy the earnest of our inheritance (Ephesians 1:14), but there is coming a day when we'll have it all—perfect health, complete provision, and eternal life.

It is difficult to comprehend how amazing our inheritance is until you consider how wonderful is the baptism of the Holy Spirit. If something this good is just the earnest or down payment of our inheritance, what must the rest be like? All of this is made possible, of course, by the fact that you are the child of God. God made sure this would be a reality in two different ways. First, we are His children by birth (John 3:5)—the new birth. Second, we are adopted into His family (Galatians 4:5). Through the new birth and the grace of God in adopting us, we are without question the children of God. But are we in a position to actually enjoy the provisions of our inheritance?

Several passages of Scripture indicate it is possible to be a believer and yet be a spiritual infant. The recipients of the letter to the Hebrews were described as needing milk and unable to handle strong meat (Hebrews 5:12, 14). This spiritual immaturity is all too common. But when it comes to enjoying the provisions of our rightful inheritance, we are not considered spiritual babies. It seems we are placed into the family of God as full-grown children.

> Now I say, That the heir, as long as he is a child, differeth nothing from a servant, though he be lord of all; But is under tutors and governors until the time appointed of the father. Even so we, when we were children, were in bondage under the elements of the world: But when the fulness of the time was come, God sent forth his Son, made of a woman, made under the law, To redeem them that were under the law, that we might receive the adoption of sons. And because ye are sons, God hath sent forth the Spirit of his Son into your hearts, crying, Abba, Father. Wherefore thou art no more a servant, but a son; and if a son, then an heir of God through Christ. (Galatians 4:1-7)

Young children in the first century did not enjoy the full provisions of their inheritance. They were required to spend years under the tutelage of a schoolmaster until they reached the appropriate age. These children were considered little more than servants. But Paul says this is not the situation for the children of God. We are not servants. We are the sons and daughters of God and have already been given the earnest of our inheritance (Ephesians 1:14). This means we can enjoy many of the benefits now. On the basis of our relationship to God as his children we are the recipients of spiritual blessings now (Ephesians 1:3) and by suffering with Him in this life we are promised to share in His glory in the future (2 Timothy 2:12; 1 Peter 4:13; 5:10). We are already sitting together in heavenly places in Christ Jesus (Ephesians 2:6) and will spend eternity reigning with Him (2 Timothy 2:12).

What you have just read is a description of a theological reality. But it is also an emotional difficulty. God's declaration over your life is often contradicted by your feelings. But you are not the child of God because you feel like it. You are the child of God because you have put your faith in Him. "For ye are all the children of God by faith in Christ Jesus" (Galatians 3:26). As the children of God, it is once again possible to fulfill God's eternal purpose for your life—to be just like Jesus (Romans 8:29). In most cases, an adopted child will not bear the physical characteristics of the adoptive parents. In fact, similarities beyond the superficial may be completely absent. Does our adoption make it more difficult for us to become like Jesus? Not when you consider that we are also born into the family of God. You can be just like Him because you have been born again by His Spirit. Through adoption and the new birth you have a new identity, a new life, and a new family. People will now be able to look at you and say, "I can see your dad in you!"

Identity Confession

I am not who Satan says I am.
I am not who others say I am.
I am not who I think or feel I am.
I am who God declares me to be.
And God has declared me to be His child.

CHAPTER 5
A New Creation

2 Corinthians 5:17
Therefore, if anyone is in Christ, he is a new creation; old things have passed away; behold, all things have become new. (NKJV)

2 Corinthians 5:17
Therefore if any person is [ingrafted] in Christ (the Messiah) he is a new creation (a new creature altogether); the old [previous moral and spiritual condition] has passed away. Behold, the fresh and new has come! (Amplified Bible)

You can probably look back at your life and point to a specific time and place where you were radically changed. You don't go to certain places you used to go. You don't say certain things you used to say. You don't do certain things you used to do. Values you used to hold have been discarded and, in their place, you have a whole new set of values, behaviors, and thoughts. For you, this change may or may not have involved thunder, lightening, or swinging from chandeliers. But for some believers, the change is quite dramatic.

Paul's original career included holding coats for the stoning of Stephen, persecuting Christian men, women, and children in Jerusalem, and developing a harassment program he intended to start in Damascus. God had other plans. In a blinding flash of light and with a thunderous voice, God extended grace to the enthusiastic tormentor. Paul fell to the ground, asked for revelation, and God obliged (Acts 9:3-5). When Paul rose to his feet, he was a different man. Although he was temporarily blind, he was seeing things more clearly than he ever had before. Several days later, Paul was a new creation and the possessor of the born again identity.

Most of us can point back to choices we wish we had never made, words we had never spoken, and things we had never done. But the capacity for sin did not originate with us. It was passed down to us from our ancestors all the way back to Adam.

> Wherefore, as by one man sin entered into the world, and death by sin; and so death passed upon all men, for that all have sinned: (Romans 5:12)

You were born with a sin nature. It is not your fault. It is not your parents' fault. Many people try to blame Eve for the human predicament, but Paul placed the blame for the sin nature squarely on the shoulders of Adam. The sin nature Adam passed on to you predisposes you to sin. In other words, it makes it easy for you to make the wrong choices and do the wrong things. Sin doesn't have to be taught. Every child can and will eventually lie, whether that behavior has been modeled for them or not. It's in their nature.

Paul uses the language of slavery in describing sin, saying we "were the servants of sin" (Romans 6:17). In other words, we had no choice in the matter. Sin was our master and we did whatever we were told to do. That was the human condition before the cross of Jesus Christ. Human beings still have the sin nature, but the power of sin has been broken and a person with the born again identity can now choose to yield to God rather than sin (Romans 6:16).

We sin because we have a sin nature, but we also sin because it is fun. A Christian who tries to convince you that sin is not fun is doing you a disservice. The Bible tells us sin is enjoyable. Moses chose not to participate in the "pleasure of sin" (Hebrews 11:25), but the point is that sin is as pleasurable as it is temporary. Consequently, we make the choice to sin. It is imperative to understand that we sin because we have a sin nature and that we sin because we make the choice to sin. In other words, we are sinners by birth and we are sinners by behavior. This helps us realize the ancient origin of the problem and our personal responsibility for it as well.

Sin forced us to live according to an identity God never intended for His children, but God was not willing to leave us in that condition. Consequently, an ancient plan—in place from the foundation of the world (1 Peter 1:19-20; Revelation 13:8)—was put into action. Because we could never do what was necessary to work our way out or buy our way out of that dilemma, God stepped into the situation and took care of it for us.

In truth, our destiny should have been the cross. Sin is rebellion against God and worthy of death (Romans 6:23). Unfortunately, our death would have accomplished nothing more than fulfilling the requirements of the Law of Moses for judgment. Eternal life would still be unavailable. So God took on human existence and, in the person of Jesus Christ, took our place on the cross. Through His death, He returned to us a privilege we lost in the Garden of Eden—the privilege of standing before God in absolute righteousness. Paul described this process in his second epistle to the church at Corinth. "For he hath made him to be sin for us, who knew no sin; that we might be made the righteousness of God in him" (2 Corinthians 5:21). If you possess the born again identity, you are the righteousness of God. Jesus became sin. Through the new birth, we became righteous. This is the ultimate example that life in a fallen world is not fair. Jesus had no reason to die. We had no right to live. He had never committed a sin. We are incapable of purely righteous actions. Yet, He became sin and through the new birth you are now righteous.

You may not feel righteous, but your feelings are often misguided. How many times have you heard a noise during the night and suspected someone was prowling through your house? You stopped breathing, felt your pulse pounding in your ears, and tried to listen intently for the next sound. But when you finally pulled together enough courage to slip out of bed, you found the house as free from intruders as it had been when you went to sleep. Our feelings are not always trustworthy. The Word of God, however, is absolutely trustworthy. It was God's idea to give you the gift of eternal life (John 3:16; Romans 6:23). Even though you have sinned in the past and may still occasionally fall (Romans 3:23), you have been justified through the blood of Jesus Christ (Romans 3:22-25) and can stand before God in total confidence. The confidence, of course, does not reside in you. It resides in the work of Jesus Christ on the cross. This is why I say your feelings don't matter. Everyone feels like a failure at times.

Everyone experiences doubts based on emotional lows and feels the occasional surge of faith in connection with emotional highs. Fortunately, we have been given something more stable than feelings or any other sensory experience—a "more sure word" (2 Peter 1:19), referring to the Scripture (2 Peter 1:20). Your feelings may suggest otherwise, but God's Word declares you to be righteous.

Through the new birth, you have the opportunity to take on a new identity. You literally become a new creation, "a new creature altogether" (2 Corinthians 5:17, Amplified Bible). As sin was placed on Jesus, you were placed in Him. "Therefore, if anyone is in Christ, he is a new creation; old things have passed away; behold, all things have become new" (2 Corinthians 5:17). So, if you are the possessor of the born again identity, what can you expect for your life? What does it mean to be a new creation?

No Condemnation

Many Christians live in a vicious vortex of shame and guilt. They have no problem believing the cross of Jesus Christ took care of every sin they committed prior to conversion, but they are fully aware they have been much less than perfect since that time. For some reason, believers often set extremely high standards of perfection for themselves. Their initial experience at an altar of forgiveness was undoubtedly characterized by true humility, repentance, and the knowledge that the grace of God was their only hope. However, this time of spiritual vulnerability and transformation is often followed by outlandish promises of immediate and total change in every area of their life, and Satan uses this enthusiastic spiritual commitment to set the trap of condemnation for the newly converted. When we repent trusting in grace and then make promises trusting in self, we are walking a path strewn with spiritual landmines. Paul's encouragement to the church at Rome is not based on the idea that believers never sin. Instead, it reveals one of the characteristics of the born again identity.

> There is therefore now no condemnation to them which are in Christ Jesus, who walk not after the flesh, but after the Spirit. (Romans 8:1)

If you are in Christ, you are a new creation. If you are a new creation, you do not have to put up with condemnation. The Holy Spirit will convict you, but never condemn you. Conviction is the prompting you receive from the Holy Spirit that encourages us to deal with a specific issue in your life. Conviction can be gentle or intense, but it will always be accompanied by hope. Condemnation, on the other hand, is a harsh, general denouncement of you as a failure and offers you nothing but despair.

Many believers are actually doubters in this area. They just cannot allow themselves to feel forgiven when they sin. You might say, "But, I still sin! How can I feel righteous when I know I repeatedly fail?" Paul did not say, "There is therefore now no chance you will ever sin again." He knew believers would sin. He was reminding us that the sin problem was taken care of by Jesus Christ and, because we are in Him, we are no longer viable targets for condemnation. Your position of right-standing with God is not based on your perfection. It is based on His.

The tension between sin in the life of the believer and the challenge to trust in the work of Jesus Christ as the basis for right-standing with God often leads to paranoid, unstable Christians. They feel saved on Sunday and lost on Monday. But God never intended for this kind of spiritual instability to characterize the life of a Christian. You have been declared to be the righteousness of God and He wants you to enjoy the benefits of that position. Some Christians get jittery when they hear these concepts. I can almost hear them say, "But you're minimizing how horrible it is when I sin!" My response: "You are minimizing how powerful the cross is when you doubt!" The Word of

God is either true or false. It is either trustworthy or it is worthy of nothing. I think I can guess which of these you believe. If you are in Christ—if you are the possessor of the born again identity—you do not have to put up with condemnation.

No Fear

Another great characteristic of the born again identity is freedom from fear. "For God hath not given us the spirit of fear; but of power, and of love, and of a sound mind" (2 Timothy 1:7). Fear in this case probably means cowardice or timidity (Newman, 2000). If you are living in fear, you are not fully appropriating the blessings of the born again identity.

Fear is sometimes grounded in the feeling that things are out of your control. You feel you don't have the power to cope with the enemy or your circumstances. But the born again identity includes all the power you need to face both. Jesus said,

> I beheld Satan as lightning fall from heaven. Behold, I give unto you power to tread on serpents and scorpions, and over all the power of the enemy: and nothing shall by any means hurt you. (Luke 10:18-19)

Notice that this promise was given to the disciples before they had received the gift of the Holy Spirit. In fact, they were given the power to cleanse lepers, heal the sick, cast out evil spirits, and even raise the dead before they had been baptized in the Spirit (Matthew 10:1, 8). All of this power was given to them freely and when they returned from one of their ministry expeditions, they gave glowing reports of the miracles that had taken place (Luke 10:17). All of this occurred prior to the outpouring of the Spirit on the day of Pentecost (Acts 2:1-4), but before His ascension Jesus promised the disciples another infusion of power. "But ye shall receive power, after that the Holy Ghost is come upon you" (Acts 1:8). This is interesting when you consider the power they already had. Now consider that if you are born again, you have been given all of the power the early church was given. Can you see how fear has no chance in the life of someone with the born again identity?

Another reason people experience fear is related to their relationships. They may feel unloved by family, friends, or even God. Fear arises when individuals experience rejection, loneliness, or anticipate either. But the born again identity brings with it an experience with love to such a degree that fear is unable to remain. God absolutely loves you and He gives you the ability to love Him and others. Consequently, fear has no power over you. "There is no fear in love; but perfect love casteth out fear" (1 John 4:18).

Fear is also related to your thoughts. When you allow your mind to conjure up erratic and frightening images it leads to unfortunate choices. But Paul promised the possessor of the born again identity a sound mind, which probably refers to the ability to control your thoughts with the intent of making sound decisions.

You do not have to be controlled by fear. God has given you all the power you will ever need, all the love you can contain, and the ability to cast down your imaginations and "every high thing that exalteth itself against the knowledge of God" (2 Corinthians 10:5) and to take control of every thought.

No Anxiety

According to the National Institute of Mental Health (2004), more than "19 million adult Americans ages 18 to 54 have anxiety disorders" (¶ 1). Stressful situations often induce anxiety, but when the anxiety becomes disproportionate to the stress it can be destructive. One of the benefits of the born again identity is freedom from harmful anxiety. Paul instructed the church at Philippi to be "careful for nothing; but in everything by prayer and supplication with thanksgiving let your requests be made known unto God" (Philippians 4:6). I like the paraphrase of that verse in *The Message*. "Don't fret or worry. Instead of worrying, pray. Let petitions and praises shape your worries into prayers, letting God know your concerns."

You have been given a resource that helps reduce or even avoid destructive anxiety. You don't have to worry or fret or be anxious about anything, because you have been given the privilege of communicating with God in prayer and supplication about whatever situation you are facing. So, as Paul said, "Instead of worrying, pray!" The result? Peace. Not just any peace, but the peace of God "which passeth all understanding shall keep your hearts and minds through Christ Jesus" (Philippians 4:7). In the place of anxiety about the past, present or future, God gives you peace.

No Defeat

Another great benefit of the born again identity is the promise of ultimate victory. The Word of God is filled with descriptions of the victory you can expect if you possess the born again identity.

> Who shall separate us from the love of Christ? shall tribulation, or distress, or persecution, or famine, or nakedness, or peril, or sword? As it is written, For thy sake we are killed all the day long; we are accounted as sheep for the slaughter. Nay, in all these things we are more than conquerors through him that loved us. (Romans 8:35-37)

> For whatsoever is born of God overcometh the world: and this is the victory that overcometh the world, even our faith. (1 John 5:4)

> Ye are of God, little children, and have overcome them: because greater is he that is in you, than he that is in the world. (1 John 4:4)

> But thanks be to God, which giveth us the victory through our Lord Jesus Christ. (1 Corinthians 15:57)

Defeat for the believer is a matter of perception. The temporary difficulties we all face are sometimes interpreted as the successful attempts of the enemy to defeat us. But defeat is a concept that goes beyond the parameters of our temporary trials. It is to be expected that you will experience trouble in this life (John 16:33), but this is not defeat. Defeat is when the battle is over and you are on the losing side. Defeat is when you give up. Defeat is when there is no hope. But the battle is not over, you are not going to give up, and there is hope. If you are born again and your faith is in Jesus Christ, you are victorious. Sin has no power over you and the devil has no rights in your life. You may experience temporary setbacks, but ultimately you are victorious.

No Curse

When Adam and Eve sinned, they experienced the tragic consequences of the curse of God. Not only were they driven out of the Garden of Eden, but each also received an individualized penalty. Adam was cursed with a lifetime of hard work. Eve was cursed with extraordinary pain in connection with childbirth. They both experienced separation from God. The implications of this curse have been passed down to all generations, but this curse does not stand alone. The Law of Moses included a curse for anyone who broke any or all of the commandments. In fact, according to James, if you broke even one of the commandments, you were guilty of breaking them all (James 2:10). Obviously, if we were still under the Law of Moses, we would be guilty of the whole law because each of us has broken at least one of the commandments. But the curse does not apply if you have the born again identity, because "Christ hath redeemed us form the curse of the law, being made a curse for us" (Galatians 3:13). In fact, quite the opposite is true. Instead of a curse, you have been blessed "with all spiritual blessings in heavenly places in Christ" (Ephesians 1:3).

No Lack

Paul made it clear that believers can expect God to supply all their needs "according to his riches in glory by Christ Jesus" (Philippians 4:19). But what, exactly, do believers truly need? The Christian world is saturated with "get-rich-quick" philosophies. According to these ideas, you can give your way to prosperity. This teaching requires hermeneutical twisting a human contortionist would be proud of. The Word of God never promises believers an abundance of financial wealth. It is certainly no sin to be wealthy, although wealth does create an environment of temptation which makes it more difficult to be saved (Matthew 19:23). But we need to consider carefully the passages of Scripture in the New Testament related to the provision God promises believers. It is clear that our needs will be met if we place the kingdom of God as number one on our priority list (Matthew 6:33), but the needs mentioned in this passage include something to eat, something to drink, and something to wear. No promise is made of houses, land, cars, or sizable bank accounts. You have to be careful when interpreting verses like Matthew 19:29.

> And every one that hath forsaken houses, or brethren, or sisters, or father, or mother, or wife, or children, or lands, for my name's sake, shall receive an hundredfold, and shall inherit everlasting life.

Most of us would be okay with receiving a hundredfold (or 100 times) the amount of houses or lands we had sacrificed. But I'm not sure we would be so willing to receive that return in brothers, sisters, fathers, and mothers. I know for a fact I am intended to only have one wife and the two children I have are plenty, thank you! The point of Jesus' statement is that someone who makes sacrifices for the Lord in this life will not go unrewarded. You'll have new resources, relationships, and even eternal life. For some reason, we want to assume that financial giving produces financial harvests, but this is not always the case. In fact, in Mark's account, he quotes Jesus as saying, "he shall receive an hundredfold now in this time, houses, and brethren, and sisters, and mothers, and children, and lands, with persecutions" (Mark 10:30). We don't like to talk about that kind of harvest. That fact is that Paul was pretty clear that the result of giving financially is often a spiritual reward.

> But this I say, He which soweth sparingly shall reap also sparingly; and he which soweth bountifully shall reap also bountifully. Every man according as he purposeth in his heart, so let him give; not grudgingly, or of necessity: for God loveth a cheerful giver. And God is able to make all grace abound toward you; that ye, always having all sufficiency in all things, may abound to every good work: (2 Corinthians 9:6-8)

These verses are sometimes taken to mean that if you will sow a financial seed, you will reap a financial harvest. The logical deduction, then, is that if you will sow a bountiful financial seed, you will reap a bountiful financial harvest. But in this passage, Paul indicates that financial sowing will result in a harvest of grace and righteousness. Even the classic verse sometimes misinterpreted to suggest financial prosperity is a reference to something other than money.

> Judge not, and ye shall not be judged: condemn not, and ye shall not be condemned: forgive, and ye shall be forgiven: Give, and it shall be given unto you; good measure, pressed down, and shaken together, and running over, shall men give into your bosom. For with the same measure that ye mete withal it shall be measured to you again. (Luke 6:27-28)

In this passage, Jesus is explaining that when you offer mercy or forgiveness you can expect to receive it back in greater quantities. There is no suggestion or promise of financial prosperity. This is not to say that principles of sowing and reaping cannot be applied in the believer's life, but financial abundance is never promised in the New Covenant. What is promised is that your every need would be met. We can take this to mean physical, mental, social, emotional, spiritual, and financial needs. But what we need and what we think we need may be two very different things. There are many places on the earth where you can survive without a car, house, or even a traditional job. I'm not suggesting that you try to do this. But I am convinced that the poorest tribesman in Africa can be spiritually blessed and rejoice that his every need is met in the same way that an American Christian businessman can when he closes a deal. The issue at stake is what you truly need. As a possessor of the born again identity, you can rest assured that your every need is met in Jesus Christ.

No Sickness, Disease, or Death

The born again identity includes freedom from sickness, disease, and death. This may seem a strange statement at first glance. We all know believers who experience sickness and disease. We certainly know believers who have died. So how can this statement be true? Peter claimed our healing has been accomplished by the stripes Jesus took upon His back (1 Peter 2:24), so how do we deal with the incongruence when believers experience sickness, disease, or death? The answer to this dilemma is found in the relationship between time and eternity. Our ultimate destiny is glorification. We will be changed from corruptible to incorruption and from mortality to immortality (1 Corinthians 15:53-55). When we have been transformed, there will be no sin, sickness, disease, depression, sorrow, or death. Until that day, God allows us to bring into the present elements of our future. Remember, the Holy Spirit has been given to us as a small portion of our entire inheritance.

> In whom ye also trusted, after that ye heard the word of truth, the gospel of your salvation: in whom also after that ye believed, ye were sealed with that holy Spirit of promise, Which is the earnest of our inheritance until the redemption of the purchased possession, unto the praise of his glory. Wherefore I also, after I heard of your faith in the Lord Jesus, and love unto all the saints. (Ephesians 1:13-15)

In other words, as wonderful as the Spirit of God is in our life, it is just the beginning. When you are sick, you can experience healing right now. But in that day, you will be healed for eternity. If you contract a disease, you can be delivered right now. But in that day, you will be delivered for eternity. You may die, but in that day, you will live forever. What we experience now is a small fraction of what we will experience in eternity. Even Lazarus, who was raised from the dead (John 11), eventually died a natural death again. He had experienced to a degree the resurrection power of Jesus Christ. In the life to come, however, he would experience that power with no restriction. Believers who experience healing now may find themselves wrestling with sickness again at some point in the future, but one day they will wrestle no more because they will be healed for eternity. That is how I can say the born again identity frees you from sickness, disease, and death. Now, you get a taste. Then, you receive it all.

The benefits of the born again identity include no condemnation, no fear, no anxiety, no defeat, no curse, no lack, and no sickness, disease, or death. You are the recipient of incredible promises from God and through those promises you are a "partaker of the divine nature" (2 Peter 1:4).

Identity Confession

I am not who Satan says I am.
I am not who others say I am.
I am not who I think or feel I am.
I am who God declares me to be.
I am a new creation in Christ Jesus.
Old things are passed away.
All things are become new.

There is no condemnation that can overwhelm me!
There is no fear that can terrify me!
There is no anxiety that can shake me!
There is no defeat that can overcome me!
There is no curse that can affect me!
There is no lack that can be experienced by me!
There is no sickness, disease, or death that can be applied to me!
I am a new creation in Christ Jesus
and I am what God declares me to be!

References

Barclay-Newman Greek Dictionary, BibleWorks for Windows, ver. 4.0.035p (3549), (c) 1998 BibleWorks, LLC.

NIMH (2004). *Anxiety disorders research at the National Institute of Mental Health*. Retrieved October 1, 2005 from http://www.nimh.nih.gov/publicat/anxresfact.cfm.

CHAPTER 6
The Temple of God

1 Corinthians 3:16-17
Know ye not that ye are the temple of God, and that the Spirit of God dwelleth in you? If any man defile the temple of God, him shall God destroy; for the temple of God is holy, which temple ye are.

1 Corinthians 6:18-20
Flee fornication. Every sin that a man doeth is without the body; but he that committeth fornication sinneth against his own body. What? know ye not that your body is the temple of the Holy Ghost which is in you, which ye have of God, and ye are not your own? For ye are bought with a price: therefore glorify God in your body, and in your spirit, which are God's.

If you possess the born again identity, you have been given something God always intended for you to have. At times, however, you may be tempted to look back at your previous identity and even idealize it enough to want to return to it. If so, you would simply be reenacting a drama played out by the children of Israel thousands of years ago. The chains of their slavery had barely fallen to the ground before they were thinking about going back. They just couldn't see how they would survive a wilderness journey, not to mention Pharaoh's bloodthirsty army at their heels.

They tasted a brand new fear and desired to run back to a 400-year-old pit of slavery. Trouble will do that to you. You idealize the past and desire to return to it. After all, the chains weren't all that bad. These scars on my back have almost healed already. They must not have been as severe as I thought. I mean, think about those melons we had to eat and the cucumbers, leeks, and onions (Numbers 11:5). Weren't they worth a little beating here and there? Compared to this wilderness, that was like heaven, wasn't it? Amazing! They were willing to put their children and their children's children into an environment of servitude and torture just because they felt more comfortable with their identity as slaves than they did as a free nation.

Going back to your previous identity is not an option. You were not destined for the chains of slavery to sin or the merciless whip of condemnation Satan so adeptly wields. If you have faced this temptation and even taken a few steps in the wrong direction, be encouraged! Such mistakes will not alter the course of your future unless you let them. God's plan for you is to live out the born again identity with purpose and power. By now, you have realized that you are the child of God. You understand that you are a new creation in Christ. But if you want to fully appropriate the blessing of God and His purpose for your life, it is essential to understand that you are also the temple of God (1 Corinthians 3:16-17; 6:18-20). This has always been God's intention for your life.

God's Eternal Desire

From the beginning of creation, God planned to have an intimate relationship with human beings. In the Garden of Eden, God frequently spoke to Adam and Eve (Genesis 1-3). It is clear God wanted mankind to enjoy the benefits of His presence and Adam and Eve experienced all of these blessings. But when they gave in to the deception of the devil, their desire for intimacy with God was impacted. As a result, they wanted to get as far away from God as possible. That's what sin does to you. It makes you want to flee from the presence of God.

> And they heard the voice of the LORD God walking in the garden in the cool of the day: and Adam and his wife hid themselves from the presence of the LORD God amongst the trees of the garden. (Genesis 3:8)

As a result of their sin, Adam and Eve experienced spiritual death (separation from God) and were removed from the Garden of Eden. They eventually had two sons and their newly acquired sin nature was passed on to them. Cain, the eldest, rose up one day in a fit of jealous rage and murdered his brother, Abel. In this story, we find one of the saddest verses in the Bible: "And Cain went out from the presence of the Lord" (Genesis 4:16).

God never wanted people to be isolated from His presence. In fact, it is clear the presence of God was the source of life in man, for God "breathed into his nostrils the breath of life; and man became a living soul" (Genesis 2:7). Thankfully, the sin of Adam and Eve did not frustrate the plan and purpose of God. He raised up a nation through Abraham's grandson, Jacob, that would usher in the advent of the Messiah.

Jacob's name was later changed to Israel and his would be the family line through which the Messiah would enter the world. God's plan was that the Messiah would take care of the sin problem and once again make God's presence completely available to mankind. Unfortunately, even though they had been chosen by God to bring the Messiah to the world, Israel often failed God. They were surrounded by heathen nations who practiced idolatry and Israel frequently mimicked their pagan religious practices. Soon after Israel's deliverance from slavery, Moses went up into a mountain to be in God's presence and receive direction for the nation's future. During his prolonged absence, the people began to demand that a golden calf be forged to give them something visible to worship. You know the rest of the story. Moses returned, saw the idolatrous worship, and broke the tablets of stone as a sign of God's anger against Israel. Not long after this occurred, God gave instructions to Moses to build the Ark of the Covenant as a visible reminder that the presence of God was with His people. I could be wrong, but it is my opinion that God might never have required the Ark if the people were not so susceptible to idolatry. But the Ark became an integral part of their existence. It was usually housed in the tabernacle, but it was instrumental in leading them to the places God wanted them to go (Numbers 10:33). It helped in the crossing of the Jordan River (Joshua 3). It played a vital role in the defeat of Jericho (Joshua 4). It served as a central gathering place for the leaders of Israel to pray (Joshua 7-8). In fact, the entire nation prayed together in the vicinity of the Ark (Judges 20:27). When the Ark of the Covenant was around, the children of Israel knew the presence of God was with them. When the Ark was around, they had joy, victory, direction, forgiveness, and power.

An analysis of Israel's history might lead you to believe the Ark of the Covenant would be a permanent religious fixture. But Jeremiah prophesied of a time when the Ark would not longer be a part of their worship.

> And I will give you pastors according to mine heart, which shall feed you with knowledge and understanding. And it shall come to pass, when ye be multiplied and increased in the land, in those days, saith the LORD, they shall say no more, The ark of the covenant of the LORD: neither shall it come to mind: neither shall they remember it; neither shall they visit it; neither shall that be done any more. (Jeremiah 3:15-16)

The Ark of the Covenant would be extracted from their religious rituals so completely they wouldn't visit it or even think about it. God never wanted a relationship with man based on visible crutches or tangible possessions. God's reason for the Ark of the Covenant, the tabernacle, and the temple was to help Israel approach Him and experience His presence. But Israel lost reverence for the Ark and eventually came to rely on it for a quick fix when they were in trouble. God did not want the people of Israel to depend on a visible Ark. He did not want the people of Israel to trust in a tabernacle made of skins or a temple made with stones. He wanted them to enjoy His literal presence, not some finite symbol of His infinite Spirit. God inspired Jeremiah to prophesy, "There is coming a day when you won't be impressed by the Ark any longer!" Ezekiel, under the inspiration of the Holy Spirit, revealed God's eternal desire.

> And I will give them one heart, and I will put a new spirit within you; and I will take the stony heart out of their flesh, and will give them an heart of flesh: (Ezekiel 11:19)

> A new heart also will I give you, and a new spirit will I put within you: and I will take away the stony heart out of your flesh, and I will give you an heart of flesh. And I will put my spirit within you, and cause you to walk in my statutes, and ye shall keep my judgments, and do them. And ye shall dwell in the land that I gave to your fathers; and ye shall be my people, and I will be your God. (Ezekiel 36:26-28)

The prophet Joel, inspired by the same Spirit, concurred with Ezekiel.

> And it shall come to pass afterward, that I will pour out my spirit upon all flesh; and your sons and your daughters shall prophesy, your old men shall dream dreams, your young men shall see visions: And also upon the servants and upon the handmaids in those days will I pour out my spirit. (Joel 2:28-29)

In contemporary terms, God would have said something like this: "No more box! No more tent! No more temple! I want My eternal Spirit to live in you!" Hundreds of years after these prophecies, the windows of Heaven opened and mankind was given the opportunity to experience the fulfillment of God's eternal desire. It started with a small group of Israelites gathered in an upper room in the city of Jerusalem.

> And when the day of Pentecost was fully come, they were all with one accord in one place. And suddenly there came a sound from heaven as of a rushing mighty wind, and it filled all the house where they were sitting. And there appeared unto them cloven tongues like as of fire, and it sat upon each of them. And they were all filled with the Holy Ghost, and began to speak with other tongues, as the Spirit gave them utterance. (Acts 2:1-4)

When these ecstatic Israelites were asked what was going on, Peter stood up and declared that the eternal desire of God was finally being fulfilled.

> But Peter, standing up with the eleven, lifted up his voice, and said unto them, Ye men of Judaea, and all ye that dwell at Jerusalem, be this known unto you, and hearken to my words: For these are not drunken, as ye suppose, seeing it is but the third hour of the day. But this is that which was spoken by the prophet Joel; And it shall come to pass in the last days, saith God, I will pour out of my Spirit upon all flesh: and your sons and your daughters shall prophesy, and your young men shall see visions, and your old men shall dream dreams: And on my servants and on my handmaidens I will pour out in those days of my Spirit; and they shall prophesy: (Acts 2:14-18)

According to Peter, God had made His Spirit available and He wanted to inhabit the hearts of men. The Greek word for Spirit is *pneuma*, which is also translated "wind" or "breath." Once again, God wanted to breathe life into our lifeless existence. With God's Spirit within us, we don't have to rely on a box, a holy geographical location, a tent of skins, or a temple of stone. Everything the Ark brought to Israel is available to us through the Spirit of God. In fact, all of these blessings are living inside of us. His presence brings supernatural benefits.

If you have the born again identity, the Spirit of God is in you and brings you unspeakable joy. “Thou wilt show me the path of life: in thy presence is fulness of joy; at thy right hand there are pleasures for evermore” (Psalm 16:11).

If you have the born again identity, the Spirit of God is in you and makes possible a permanent relationship with God. “Surely the righteous shall give thanks unto they name: the upright shall dwell in thy presence” (Psalm 140:13).

If you have the born again identity, the Spirit of God is in you and brings with it a refreshing like you've never experienced before. “Repent ye therefore, and be converted, that your sins may be blotted out, when the times of refreshing shall come from the presence of the Lord” (Acts 3:19).

If you have the born again identity, you have been filled with the Spirit of the eternal, omniscient, omnipotent, and omnipresent God. He has promised that He would never leave you or forsake you (Hebrews 13:5). When you wake up in the morning, He is there. When you brush your teeth, comb your hair, and eat your breakfast, He is there. When you get in the car and head to work, He is there. When you drive home, eat dinner, and get ready for bed, He is there. Your circumstances are not indicators of His presence or absence. When you go through the fire, He is there. When you experience the flood, He is there. When you suffer through a trial, He is there. When you make it to the top of the mountain or struggle through the lowest valley, He is there.

God's eternal desire for your life is that His Spirit be with you, in you, above you, beneath you, and through you. He longs for you to be His—not because you have to, not because He forces you, not because of His blessings, not because you are terrified of His curses, not for hope of Heaven, and not for the fear of Hell—but because you love Him! He wants you to be one of His people and He wants to be your God.

> And I will give them an heart to know me, that I am the LORD: and they shall be my people, and I will be their God: for they shall return unto me with their whole heart. (Jeremiah 24:7)

> At the same time, saith the LORD, will I be the God of all the families of Israel, and they shall be my people. (Jeremiah 31:1)
>
> But this shall be the covenant that I will make with the house of Israel; After those days, saith the LORD, I will put my law in their inward parts, and write it in their hearts; and will be their God, and they shall be my people. (Jeremiah 31:33)
>
> And they shall be my people, and I will be their God: (Jeremiah 32:38)
>
> That they may walk in my statutes, and keep mine ordinances, and do them: and they shall be my people, and I will be their God. (Ezekiel 11:20)
>
> My tabernacle also shall be with them: yea, I will be their God, and they shall be my people. (Ezekiel 37:27)
>
> And I will bring them, and they shall dwell in the midst of Jerusalem: and they shall be my people, and I will be their God, in truth and in righteousness. (Zechariah 8:8)

The New Testament is clear that this relationship is for those of the born again identity. Anyone filled with the Spirit of God is considered by God to be His temple.

> And what agreement hath the temple of God with idols? for ye are the temple of the living God; as God hath said, I will dwell in them, and walk in them; and I will be their God, and they shall be my people. (2 Corinthians 6:16)

God's eternal desire is to be in such an intimate relationship with you that you allow Him to live within you.

It is an offer hard to resist. When God is in you, "greater is he that is in you, than he that is in the world" (1 John 4:4). Do you want joy, peace, and victory? Then let God live in you!

I have never understood people who confess faith in Jesus Christ but are unwilling to experience the infilling of the Holy Spirit. They are missing out on so much. On the other hand, if you are the possessor of the born again identity, God wants you to be an eternal temple within which His Spirit will reside for eternity.

Identity Confession

I am not who Satan says I am.
I am not who others say I am.
I am not who I think or feel I am.
I am who God declares me to be.

I am the temple of God
The Spirit of God resides within me.

CHAPTER 7
The Body of Christ

1 Corinthians 12:26-27
And whether one member suffer, all the members suffer with it; or one member be honoured, all the members rejoice with it. Now ye are the body of Christ, and members in particular.

An experience with God requires no particular physical posture. When the Holy Spirit was first poured out, the recipients were sitting (Acts 2:1-4). When Peter received a vision, he may have been lying down because the voice told him to arise (Acts 10:13). Of course, even if this reference is ambiguous, Psalm 63:6 is not. "When I remember thee upon my bed, and meditate on thee in the night watches." You can experience the presence of God kneeling, standing, sitting, walking, lying down, or any other physical posture you can think of. But if you want to fully appropriate the blessings of God and His purpose for your life, you need to carefully consider by what spiritual posture you approach Him. Sin separates us from God (Isaiah 59:2) and, even though Jesus took care of the sin problem, we are frequently tempted to approach God in less than effective ways.

The Slave

Some believers approach God as His slave. As I mentioned in Chapter 1, it is completely appropriate to consider yourself the servant of God. Paul did (Romans 1:1; Philippians 1:1; Titus 1:1). In fact, he suggested all believers were the servants of God (Romans 6:22; Ephesians 6:6). Peter agreed, advising believers to use their liberty as the servants of God (1 Peter 2:16). But there is a tremendous difference between freely choosing to yield to God as His servant and perceiving self as an unworthy slave with no right to be in His presence. One of the drawbacks to this approach is that the servant rarely knows what his master is doing (John 15:15). This mentality expects very little from God and, as a result, that expectation is usually met. God is our master and we are His servants, but He has given us the privilege of approaching Him without the posture of slavery. If you possess the born again identity, you may be the servant of God, but you can "come boldly unto the throne of grace" (Hebrews 4:16).

The Disciple

Some believers approach God as a disciple and there is nothing wrong with this approach. The original followers of

Jesus were called disciples. They embraced His teaching and were given the opportunity to minister under His authority (Matthew 10). Just before Jesus ascended into Heaven, He instructed them to make disciples of all nations (Matthew 28:19). The members of the early church were called disciples until Acts 11, when it seems residents of Antioch began to call them Christians.

Our relationship to God should include the dynamics of disciple to teacher, but this relationship alone does not provide the most effective spiritual posture for approaching God. In this relationship, the teacher still maintains distinction from the disciples and will probably not reveal everything.

The Friend

It is an incredible concept, but God desires for the relationship between Himself and humanity to be based on friendship. Abraham was called the friend of God (James 2:23) and Jesus made this a reality for his followers. In contrast to the limited revelation available to his followers as disciples, Jesus opened the door of friendship and disclosed incredible spiritual truths.

> Ye are my friends, if ye do whatsoever I command you. Henceforth I call you not servants; for the servant

> knoweth not what his lord doeth: but I have called you friends; for all things that I have heard of my Father I have made known unto you. Ye have not chosen me, but I have chosen you, and ordained you, that ye should go and bring forth fruit, and that your fruit should remain: that whatsoever ye shall ask of the Father in my name, he may give it you. (John 15:14-16)

The implications of friendship with God are clear in this passage. He chose us to be His friends. He ordained us to bring forth fruit that would last. Finally, He gave us the right to ask God for whatever we need. Friendship with God may be more effective as a spiritual posture than approaching Him as a slave or disciple, but alone it does not seem to be the most effective.

The Brother

As strange as it sounds, the Word of God is clear that the possessor of the born again identity enjoys a position as the brother of Jesus Christ. "For whom he did foreknow, he also did predestinate to be conformed to the image of his Son, that he might be the firstborn among many brethren (Romans 8:29). Through the incarnation, Jesus calls you his brother (Hebrews 2:11) and, as his brother, you are a joint-heir of God (Romans 8:17). It may be difficult to think of yourself in terms of being the sibling of Jesus, but the born again identity makes this a reality.

The Son

We have already discovered the work of Jesus Christ made it possible for believers to be restored to their rightful place as the children of God. This spiritual posture is powerful. "But as many as receive him, to them gave he power to become the sons of God" (John 1:10). If you are led by the Spirit, you are the child of God (Romans 8:14), a privilege made possible by the love of our Father (1 John 3:1-2). As the children of God, we can truly pray to our Father in Heaven (Matthew 6:9; Luke 11:2).

As a child of God, you have greater access to His presence than a slave or disciple. If someone wants to meet with me, I expect them to set up an appointment or at least have the office call me to make sure I'm available. But my children are welcome to see me at any time. I am more than happy to set aside what I am doing to spend time with them. God expects His children to walk into His presence whenever they want to and He will never fail to open His arms to receive them.

The Bride

The doctrine of the bride of Christ is not presented in any systematic way in the New Testament, but there is biblical evidence to support the idea that such a relationship with God is possible. John the Baptist referred to Jesus as the bridegroom and to himself as a friend of the bridegroom (John 3:28-29). Jesus referred to Himself as the bridegroom.

> And they said unto him, Why do the disciples of John fast often, and make prayers, and likewise the disciples of the Pharisees; but thine eat and drink? And he said unto them, Can ye make the children of the bridechamber fast, while the bridegroom is with them? But the days will come, when the bridegroom shall be taken away from them, and then shall they fast in those days. (Luke 5:33-35)

Paul compared our relationship with Jesus to that of a husband and wife.

> Submitting yourselves one to another in the fear of God. Wives, submit yourselves unto your own husbands, as unto the Lord. For the husband is the head of the wife, even as Christ is the head of the church: and he is the saviour of the body. Therefore as the church is subject unto Christ, so let the wives be to their own husbands in every thing. Husbands, love your wives, even as Christ also loved the church, and gave himself for it; (Ephesians 5:21-25)

This text is often read as offering insight for a successful marriage, and it does. But Paul intended the marriage relationship to be an analogy of an even greater spiritual reality: the relationship between Christ and the church. "This is a great mystery: but I speak concerning Christ and the church" (Ephesians 5:32). By using the word "mystery," Paul indicated that his description of marriage was meant to serve to illustrate how Christ and the church are related. One of his greatest desires was to maintain the purity of the church in expectation of her marriage to Christ.

> For I am jealous over you with godly jealousy: for I have espoused you to one husband, that I may present you as a chaste virgin to Christ (2 Corinthians 11:2).

The relationship with Christ now enjoyed by those with the born again identity will one day culminate in "the marriage supper of the Lamb" (Revelation 19:9).

Every relationship described prior to this one involves two separate individuals who remain distinct. With each, closeness is possible to some degree, but the relationship between bridegroom and bride or husband and wife by its very nature involves a deeper level of intimacy. In physical terms, a husband and wife become one flesh (Genesis 2:24; Matthew 19:5-6; Mark 10:8; 1 Corinthians 6:16; Ephesians 5:31). In spiritual terms, our relationship with Jesus as His bride involves oneness of spirit and destiny. The implications of this relationship are compelling. As the bride of Christ, believers enjoy provision, protection, and purpose. This relationship seems to be relevant for time and eternity, but is it possible there is another effective spiritual posture?

The Body

If you are the possessor of the born again identity and you limit your approach to God as a slave, a disciple, a brother, a son, or the bride, you are missing out on one of the most intimate and powerful relationships possible with God. Several passages of Scripture indicate believers are part of a spiritual entity or organism called the body of Christ.

> For the husband is the head of the wife, even as Christ is the head of the church: and he is the saviour of the body. (Ephesians 5:23)

> And he is before all things, and by him all things consist. And he is the head of the body, the church: who is the beginning, the firstborn from the dead; that in all things he might have the preeminence. For it pleased the Father that in him should all fulness dwell; (Colossians 1:17-19)

> Let no man beguile you of your reward in a voluntary humility and worshipping of angels, intruding into those things which he hath not seen, vainly puffed up by his fleshly mind, And not holding the Head, from which all the body by joints and bands having nourishment ministered, and knit together, increaseth with the increase of God. (Colossians 2:18-19)

I especially like Colossians 2:19 from *The Message*: "They're completely out of touch with the source of life, Christ, who puts us together in one piece, whose very breath and blood flow through us. He is the Head and we are the body."

Jesus Christ is the head of the body and every possessor of the born again identity is a member of that body. We are the body of Christ. Every other relationship mentioned above involves distinct individuals. Even a husband and wife, though one, still retain a degree of separation. But the relationship between the Head and the body is one of complete unity, and if that unity is maintained the results are astonishing.

In physical terms, the head is the primary location from which the central nervous system communicates with the rest of the body (the central nervous system includes the brain and the spinal cord). The peripheral nervous system, located throughout the rest of the body, sends signals back to the central nervous system through a complicated network of neural connections. If the channel of communication between the peripheral nervous system and the central nervous system is disrupted it can lead to serious health consequences, including death.

Jesus is the Head of the body. He speaks with us through His Word and His Spirit and it is vital that we communicate with Him through prayer and worship. If this connection is severed, we will ultimately face spiritual death. But if that connection remains open and communication flows freely, the body will experience spiritual health and a mind-boggling dimension of spiritual power. To better understand the implications of being the body of Christ, it is necessary to look quickly at the various ways God has revealed Himself to the world.

Through the incarnation, God took on human existence (John 1:14; 1 Timothy 3:16). The Holy Spirit overshadowed the womb of Mary and she supernaturally conceived a son (Matthew 1:18, 20; Luke 1:35). Jesus had to go through the same process of human development we all do (Luke 2:52), but when He started His ministry it was characterized by miracles, signs, and wonders. This demonstration of power was in His body even before His glorification.

After the crucifixion, the body of Jesus was buried in the borrowed tomb of Joseph of Arimathaea (Matthew 27:57-60). But He had prophesied that He would rise from the dead (John 2:19) and on the third day He did (Luke 24:46). In His glorified body, Jesus appeared to many people (1

Corinthians 15:5-8). In His glorified body, He was known to vanish (Luke 24:31). In His glorified body, Jesus passed into a room that was locked and visited with His disciples (John 20:19). In His glorified body, He performed a miracle by providing a supernatural abundance of fish to the disciples who had caught nothing all night (John 21:4-6).

Jesus demonstrated the power of God in His ministry prior to His death and after His resurrection, before and after His glorification. It is any wonder that we find the body of Christ in the Book of Acts and throughout history demonstrating the power of God in such a dynamic way? We are the body of Christ (Colossians 2:19) today. Through the provisions of the born again identity, we can approach God through this spiritual posture and see His power manifested greatly in our lives.

Identity Confession

I am not who Satan says I am.
I am not who others say I am.
I am not who I think or feel I am.
I am who God declares me to be.

I am more than a slave.
I am more than a disciple.
I am more than a friend.
I am more than a brother.
I am more than a son.
I am more than a member of the bride.
I am a member of the body of Christ.
I have a purpose and I have been given power.
I am who God has declared me to be!

CHAPTER 8
The Born Again Identity

Matthew 5:48
In a word, what I'm saying is, Grow up. You're kingdom subjects. Now live like it. Live out your God-created identity. Live generously and graciously toward others, the way God lives toward you. (The Message)

Millions of people in every nation of the world suffer from a spiritual identity crisis. They wander through life searching for purpose and direction but often fall into despair because they don't know who they are or why they exist. They seek to find their identity in their work, their family, their friendships, or their pastimes, and they end up living with constant disappointment.

God created us to live eternally as His children, but through the rebellion of Adam and Eve every human being lost that privilege. Sin marred God's perfect creation and leaves unanswered the primary question of existence: Who am I? But through the incarnation and the death, burial, and resurrection of Jesus Christ, the sin problem has been eradicated and we have been given the opportunity to once again take our rightful place as the children of God.

Satan would like for you to believe that your failures mandate a destiny of doom. He knows that you will never fully experience the blessings of God and His purpose for your life if you continue to buy into a sin-twisted identity. Satan will use every means possible—from your tendency to forget to the influence of other people in your life—to obstruct your path to this revelation. He is terrified that you might discover who God has declared you to be. Once you appropriate the born again identity, Satan's power over your life is broken. His plan for your future is thwarted. Everything he previously stole from you is restored.

As a recipient of the born again identity, you have been challenged to grow up and live out the identity God created for you (Matthew 5:48, *The Message*). God has given you all of the power you need to accomplish this. You are no longer a slave to sin. You are no longer destined for destruction. Through the born again identity, you are a new creation. You are the child of God. You are the temple of God and you are a member of the body of Christ. Your past has been taken care of. Your present is secure. Your future is certain. The implications of the born again identity are immediately pertinent and eternally relevant. You are not who Satan says you are. You are not who other say you are. You are not even necessarily who you think or feel you are. You are who God has declared you to be!

Scripture Index

1

2

A

C

E

G

H

I

J

L

M

N

P

R

T

Z

To order additional copies of this book,
please use the information below:

Born Again Ministries
9023 West Lane / Stockton, CA 95210
Telephone: 209-476-7896
Email: marksegraves@bornagainidentity.com
Website: www.bornagainidentity.com